20th CENTURY Plastic Jewelry

Roseann Ettinger

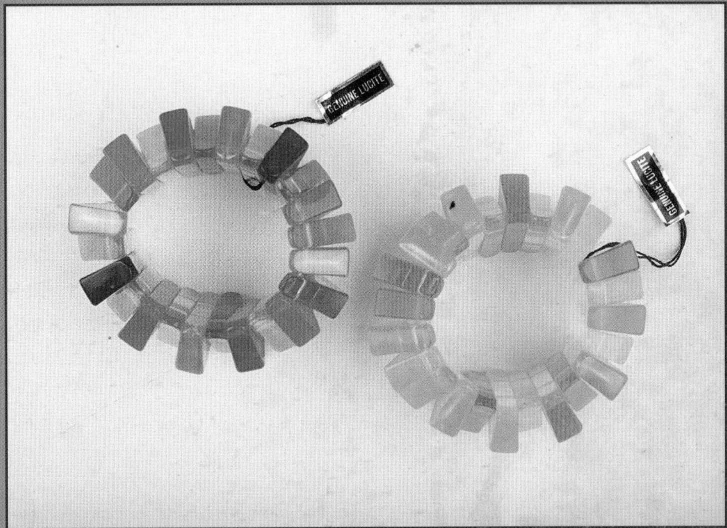

4880 Lower Valley Road Atglen, Pennsylvania 19310

Dedication

To My Family

Other Schiffer Books by Roseann Ettinger

Popular Jewelry of the '60s, '70s, & '80s
Popular Jewelry, 1840-1940
Forties & Fifties Popular Jewelry
'50s Popular Fashions
Fifties Forever! Popular Fashions for Men, Women, Boys, and Girls
Psychedelic Chic: Artistic Fashions of the Late 1960s & Early 1970s
Men's Clothing & Fabrics in the 1890s
3000 Shoes from 1896
Handbags
Trunks, Traveling Bags, and Satchels
20th Century Neckties: Pre-1955
Popular and Collectible Neckties: 1955 to the Present
Antique Dresser Sets: 1890s - 1950s
Compacts and Smoking Accessories

Library of Congress Control Number: 2006938029

Designed by John P. Cheek
Cover design by Bruce Waters
Type set in DomBold BT/ Souvenir Lt BT

ISBN: 0-7643-2612-0
Printed in China
1 2 3 4

Published by Schiffer Publishing Ltd.
4880 Lower Valley Road
Atglen, PA 19310
Phone: (610) 593-1777; Fax: (610) 593-2002
E-mail: Info@schifferbooks.com

In Europe, Schiffer books are distributed by
Bushwood Books
6 Marksbury Ave.
Kew Gardens
Surrey TW9 4JF England
Phone: 44 (0) 20 8392-8585;
Fax: 44 (0) 20 8392-9876
E-mail: info@bushwoodbooks.co.uk
Website: www.bushwoodbooks.co.uk
Free postage in the U.K., Europe; air mail at cost.

Contents

Acknowledgments

I could never thank my family enough for tolerating my passion for collecting, for not complaining when I drag them along to an antique show or flea market or for their understanding when I spend long hours researching when I could be doing something else with them. This passion is very time consuming as it has consumed much of my life the last 25 years. It is a labor of love. When a book idea pops into my head, I begin a journey devoted to finding examples for that book. My quest eventually takes me to a place where I feel that I have acquired enough examples to photograph to create the book. Most of the time it takes many years before my journey ends and I get to the point where I have collected enough examples to convey the message that I want to get across to my readers. On very rare occasions, it takes less time. Because of the broad spectrum of plastic in jewelry manufacture and design, I am confident that this book will be the first of a series because of the actual content. It was designed to tempt the palette. It was not designed to be a complete reference guide because there is so much more to learn and so much more to see. Hundreds of examples of plastic jewelry have been photographed here but thousands more are waiting to be uncovered and photographed for future books. So to my husband, Terry, and my four children: Clint, Amber, Lexie, and Sabrina, look out guys! Here I go again, for my quest never seems to end.

Thank you, Bruce Waters at Schiffer Publishing, for photographing the jewelry in this book. Last, but certainly not least, I am extremely grateful to Peter and Nancy Schiffer for believing in me and my ideas for almost 20 years.

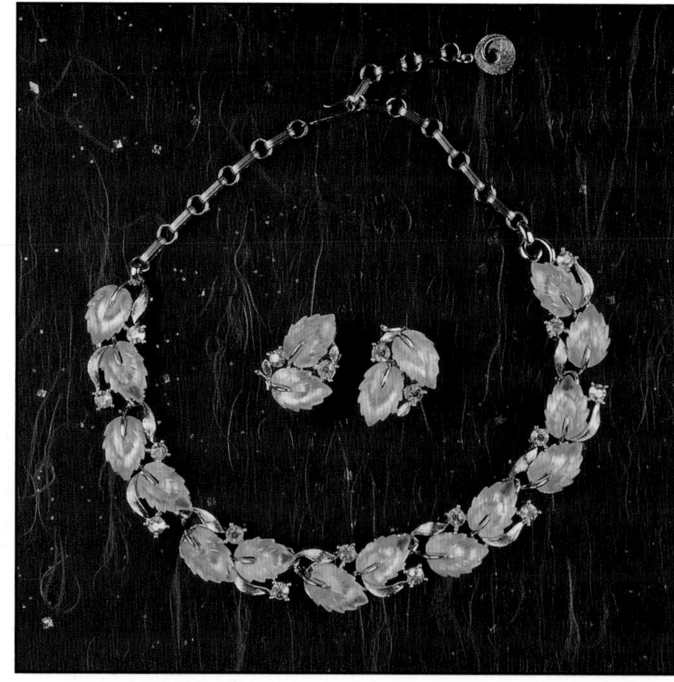

Introduction to 20th Century Plastic Jewelry

The 20th century standard of living in the developed world would not have advanced as far as it did without the advent of plastics in industry. Hundreds of manufacturers produced a variety of plastics throughout the decades of the 20th century, with many different trade names for various types of plastics. Certain plastics were cast, while others for formed with injection molding. Cast phenolics were available in sheets, rods, tubes, and even custom shapes. All plastics, whether natural or synthetic, can be referred to as a polymer.

Advertisement for DuPont Plastics by E.I. DuPont De Nemours & Co., Arlington, New Jersey, as seen in *Modern Plastics Encyclopedia*, 1949.

The plastics industry in the United States in the 20th century was huge business. In almost every aspect of daily life, plastics have touched people in one way or another. From inexpensive kitchen gadgets to fountain pens, radios, aircraft, and automobile parts, plastics have dominated almost everything about the world around us.

Examples of natural polymers are horn, tortoise shell, amber, latex, and tar. Chemically modified natural polymers began to appear in the 1800s. Celluloid can be classified as a chemically modified natural polymer since celluloid is made of cellulose, which can be obtained from wood pulp or cotton linters.

As early as 1833, the oldest synthetic polymer made of cellulose nitrate was made by Braconnot in France. By 1845, a German researcher named Schoenbein also dabbled in synthetic plastics. Alexander Parkes, in England, worked for about a decade, between 1855 and 1865, experimenting with cellulose nitrate. His polymer was called Parkesine. Early cellulose nitrate, which was patented in 1869 by John Wesley Hyatt in the United States, became known as celluloid, and was used for making ladies' decorative hair combs, hat pins, toilet articles, and dresser accessories.

Thousands of applications of thermoplastics and thermo-set plastics were used industrially as well as for home and personal use. It was only natural that jewelry manufacture became the perfect arena for utilizing this inexpensive medium for designing wonderful treasures to adorn and be adored today.

In the first half of the 20th century, architecture, furniture, sporting goods, toys, sewing notions, premiums, and advertising specialties utilized plastics in many forms. Medicine, dentistry, science, machinery, agriculture, packaging, transportation, electrical appliances, hardware, and lighting had components made of plastics. Store displays, signs, and office and photography equipment utilized plastics in their designs.

In the 1940s, store window and counter-top displays used for millinery, gloves, shoes, shirts, and jewelry were made of clear acrylic sheets and rods. Pocketknives were made of cellulose nitrate as well as Bakelite phenolic plastic. An Aunt Jemima pancake syrup pitcher, popular in the late 1940s, was made of polystyrene. Housings for fountain pens and mechanical pencils were molded of Forticel. Molded one-piece hair curlers were made of Vinylite. Toilet seats were molded from colorful Plaskon. Store mannequins were made of polyester resin. Telephones were injection molded with Butyrate, which was advertised as being a strong and economical plastic. Restaurant tableware molded from Melamine was perfect for stacking. In the late 1940s, contact lenses were made from clear acrylics.

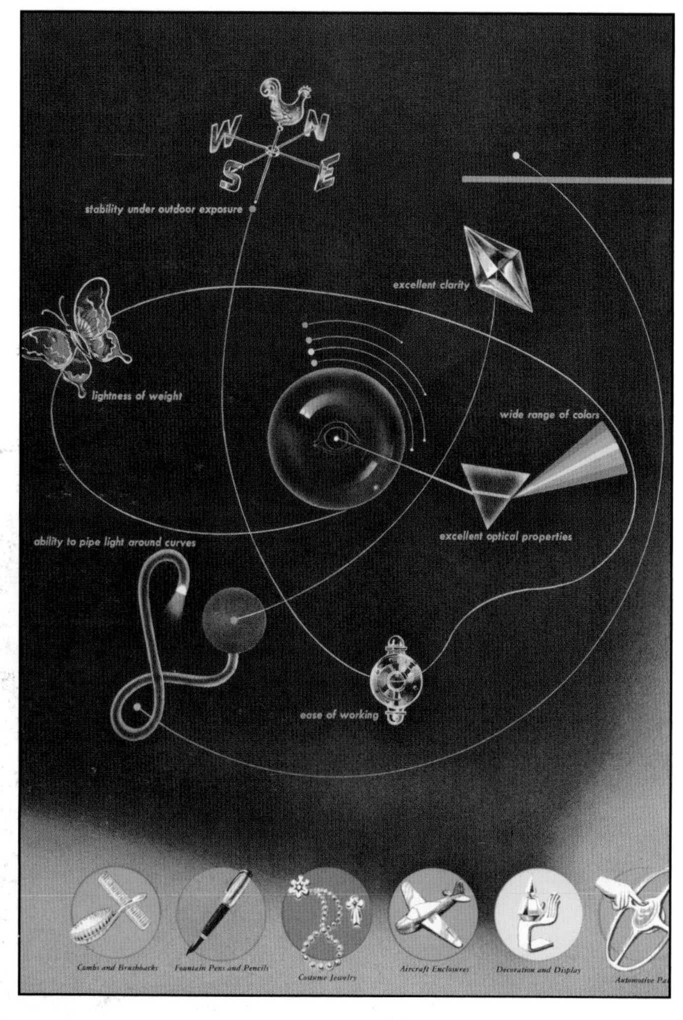

DuPont plastics advertisement showing the general characteristics of Lucite and its many applications including costume jewelry.

Advertisement for Catalin cast phenolics, molding compounds and wood adhesives as seen in *Modern Plastics Encyclopedia*, 1949.

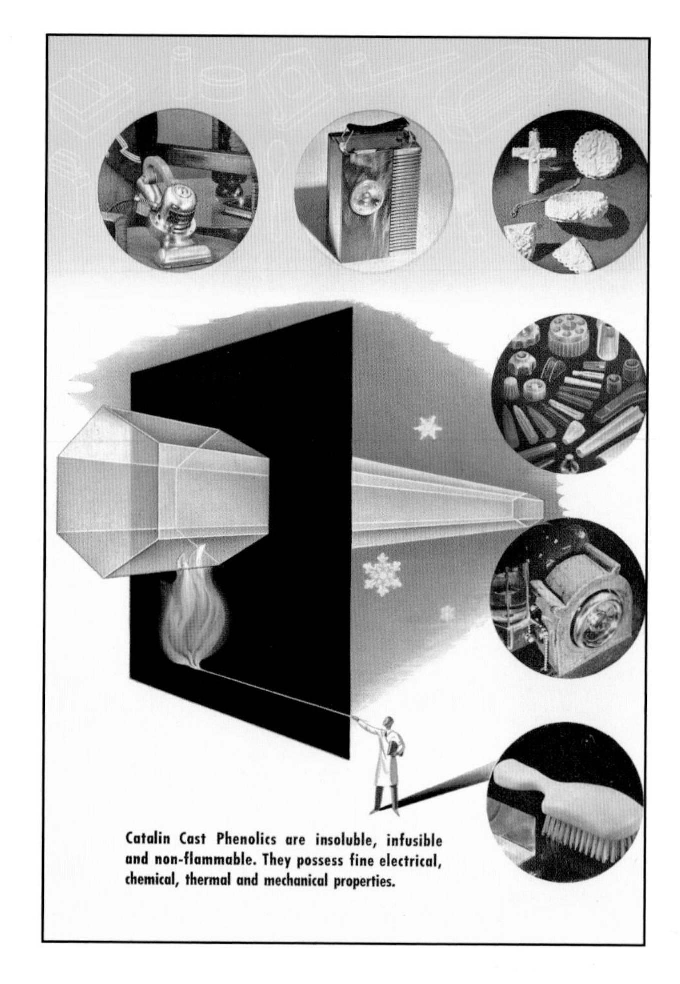

Advertisement showing Catalin cast phenolic plastics and its many applications including costume jewelry.

BAKELITE Molding Plastics
Heat-Resistant Phenolics; Special Phenolics
BAKELITE Cast Resins

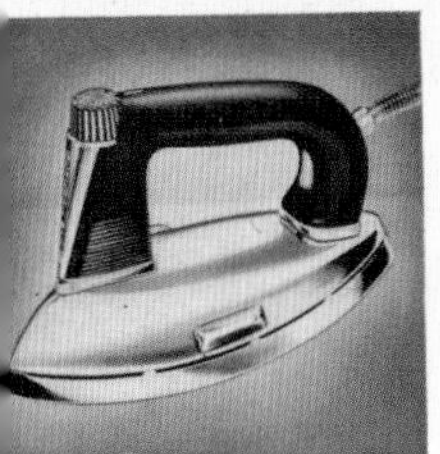
ctric iron handles, molded from BAKELITE at-Resistant Phenolics, are comfortable to the uch; provide excellent electrical insulation.

Electrical appliances, incorporating heating elements, are equipped with bases and fittings molded from BAKELITE Heat-Resistant Phenolics.

Molded from BAKELITE Heat-Resistant Phenolics kitchen utensil handles retain their attractiv appearance despite heat and frequent washing

nife handles molded from BAKELITE Phenolic olding blanks combine attractive finish with gh strength and washability.

BAKELITE Low-Loss Molding Phenolics provide outstanding electrical and physical properties for radio and other high-frequency equipment.

Heavy-duty bearings, molded from BAKELIT Low-Frictional Phenolic, have long service life effect important savings in lubrication costs.

ight in weight, necklaces and earrings of BAKE- ITE Cast Resin are attractive and always remain warm to the touch.

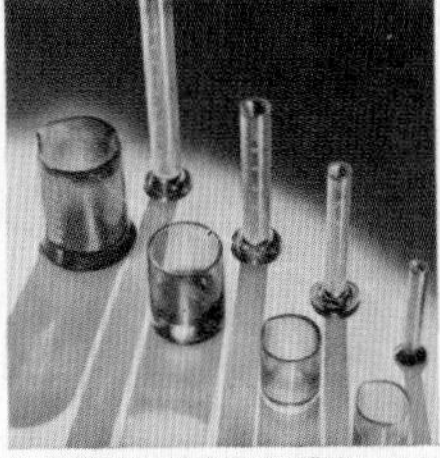
Chemical-resistant BAKELITE Cast Resins are employed for transparent laboratory ware. This equipment will withstand hydrofluoric acid.

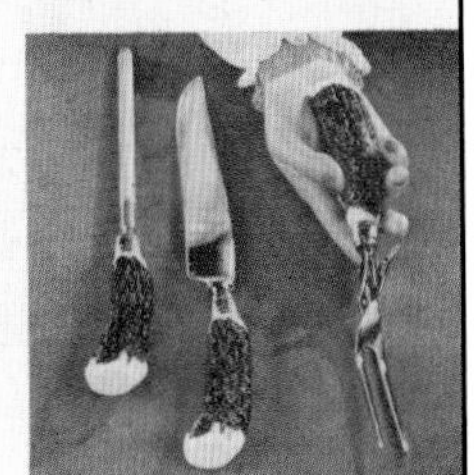
Carving sets with simulated stag handles o BAKELITE Cast Resin possess a dignified beauty offer years of practical service.

AKELITE CORPORATION

Ad by the Bakelite Corporation for Bakelite molding plastics and cast resins and its many applications including costume jewelry.

there's real gold **at the end of Koppers rainbow of plastics**

POLYSTYRENE
CELLULOSE ACETATE
ETHYL CELLULOSE

341

KOPPERS COMPANY, INC.

CHEMICAL DIVISION, MAIN OFFICE: KOPPERS BUILDING, PITTSBURGH 19, PA.

350 FIFTH AVENUE, NEW YORK 1, N. Y.
LONGACRE 4-1130

BROAD STREET STATION BUILDING, PHILADELPHIA 3, PA.
SPRUCE 4-6517

250 STUART STREET, BOSTON 16, MASS.
LIBERTY 26525

178 MASSASOIT AVENUE, EAST PROVIDENCE 14, R. I.
E. PROVIDENCE 4850

KOPPERS BUILDING, PITTSBURGH 19, PA.
ATLANTIC 6240 EXT. 689

2631 WOODWARD AVENUE, DETROIT 1, MICH.
CHERRY 3396

2040 PEOPLES GAS BUILDING, CHICAGO 3, ILL.
WEBSTER 2400

390 NINTH STREET, SAN FRANCISCO 3, CALIF.
MARKET 1-6005

659 E. GAGE AVENUE, LOS ANGELES 1, CALIF.
ADAMS 3-6231

The Koppers Company was responsible for manufacturing simulated pearls out of cellulose acetate. They *looked like the real thing, are warm to the touch, light in weight and practically unbreakable*.

Plaskon molding powder advertised in Modern Plastics Encyclopedia, 1949.

Max Factor Hollywood cosmetic make-up kit of Plaskon Molded Color. This smart case is not only an efficient housing, but a merchandising aid, as well.

THE HISTORY OF PLASKON MOLDING COMPOUNDS

The history of Plaskon is one of pioneering. At the beginning of the past quarter-century, industry was streamlining its production methods. Increasing competition demanded new designs, new materials, new fabricating techniques. One of the major objectives was the reduction of weight without the sacrifice of strength.

In 1928, the Toledo Scale Company investigated the possibilities of plastic materials for weight reduction and the improvement of the appearance of scales such as used in retail stores. To meet the need, a new fellowship at the Mellon Institute of Industrial Research in Pittsburgh was established by the Toledo Scale Company for the express purpose of developing a white plastic. Two years of pioneering . . . of endless trials and tests . . . of experimenting with new materials and new methods resulted in a molding compound with unique color possibilities. It was named Plaskon, available today in the form of urea- and melamine-formaldehyde molding compounds in a wide range of colors.

The commercial development of Plaskon in 1930 completely overcame the limitations of appearance and color which had until that time handicapped the thermosetting plastic compounds on the market. Today, Plaskon molding compounds are used for hundreds of plastic applications not only for its beautiful colors, but for the many other desirable features described in this book.

440

Max Factor Hollywood cosmetic kit and jewelry made of Plaskon thermoset plastic in 1949.

The many colors of plaskon urea-and melamine-formaldehyde fabricating material.

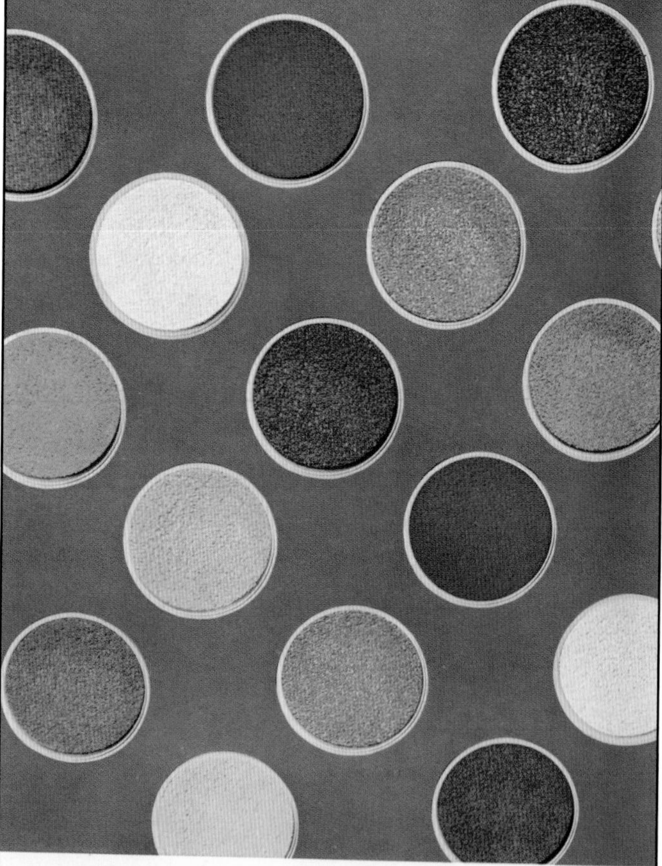

Plaskon urea- and melamine-formaldehyde plastics offer the industry versatile and colorful fabricating materials. This booklet gives a concise and pictorial explanation of what Plaskon can offer you in the development of manufacturing and merchandising opportunities.

439

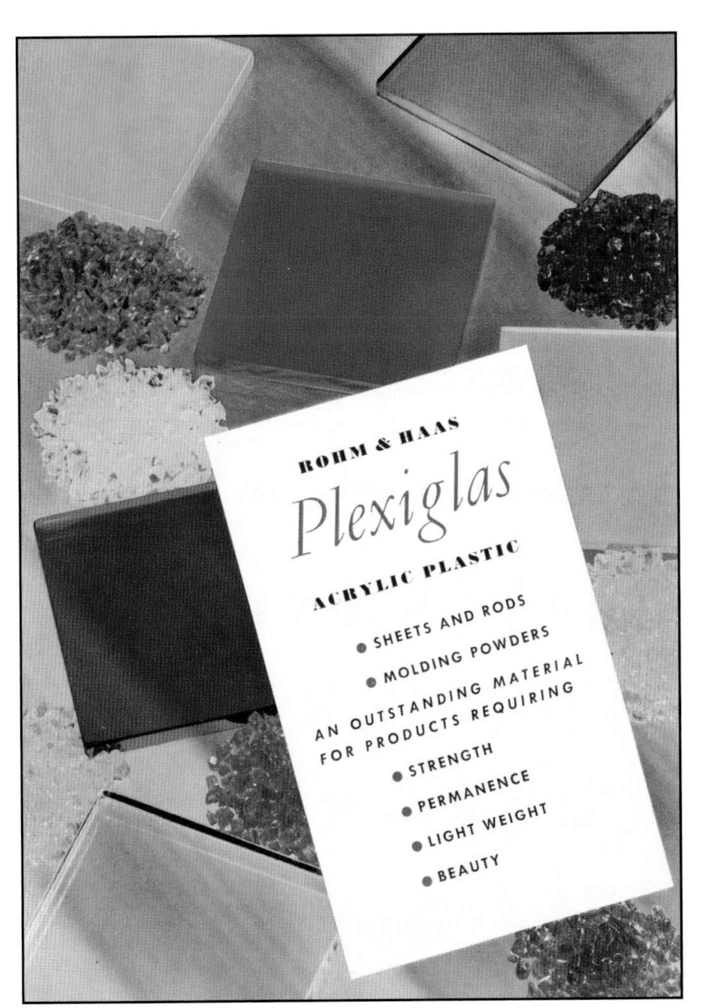

Advertisement for Rohm & Haas Plexiglas Acrylic Plastic available in sheets, rods and molding powders.

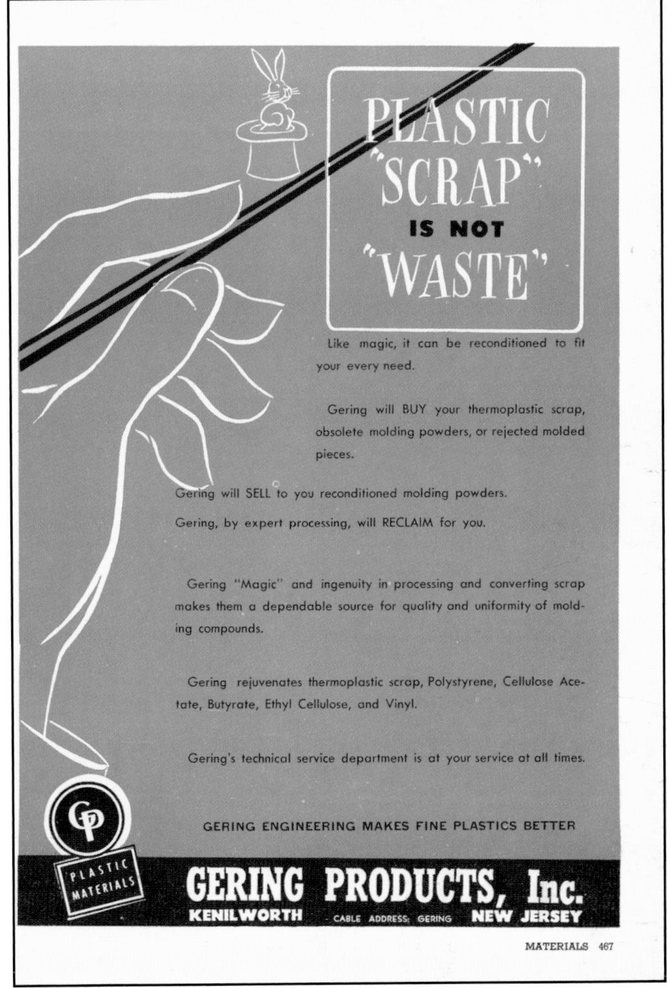

Gering Poducts, Inc. of Kenilworth, New Jersey was a plastic company that bought obsolete molding powders, thermoplastic scrap and rejected molded pieces and actually recycled them. As advertised in 1949, Gering Engineering Makes Fine Plastics Better.

Inexpensive plastic jewelry was coated with gold and silver to create a more expensive look. Mirro-Plex, Inc., New York, was one company in the late 1940s that did this type of work.

Chapter 1

Early in the Century

George F. Berkander is said to have created the first piece of hand-made celluloid jewelry in 1906 in the United States. Early plastic jewelry was made from "French Ivory," called celluloid. As technology improved, more elaborate pieces evolved.

Many different trade names were used to identify celluloid material. Ivorine, Fiberlite, Ivory Fiberloid, and Ivory Grained Celluloid were common.

Hand painted celluloid became popular as dainty clips, brooches, necklaces, and earrings made in the shapes of flower baskets and bouquets were tinted with pastel colors. Some of these were made in Japan. Wonderful costume jewelry items, in particular rhinestone-encrusted bangle bracelets, brooches, dress clips, necklaces, and more were mass-produced in the late 1920s, Art Deco period. These pieces are extremely desirable today and command high prices.

By the late 1930s, entire jewelry cases in department stores were devoted to plastic jewelry.

Two-piece belt buckle or cloak clasp, molded composition resembling gutta percha, 1870s. $145.

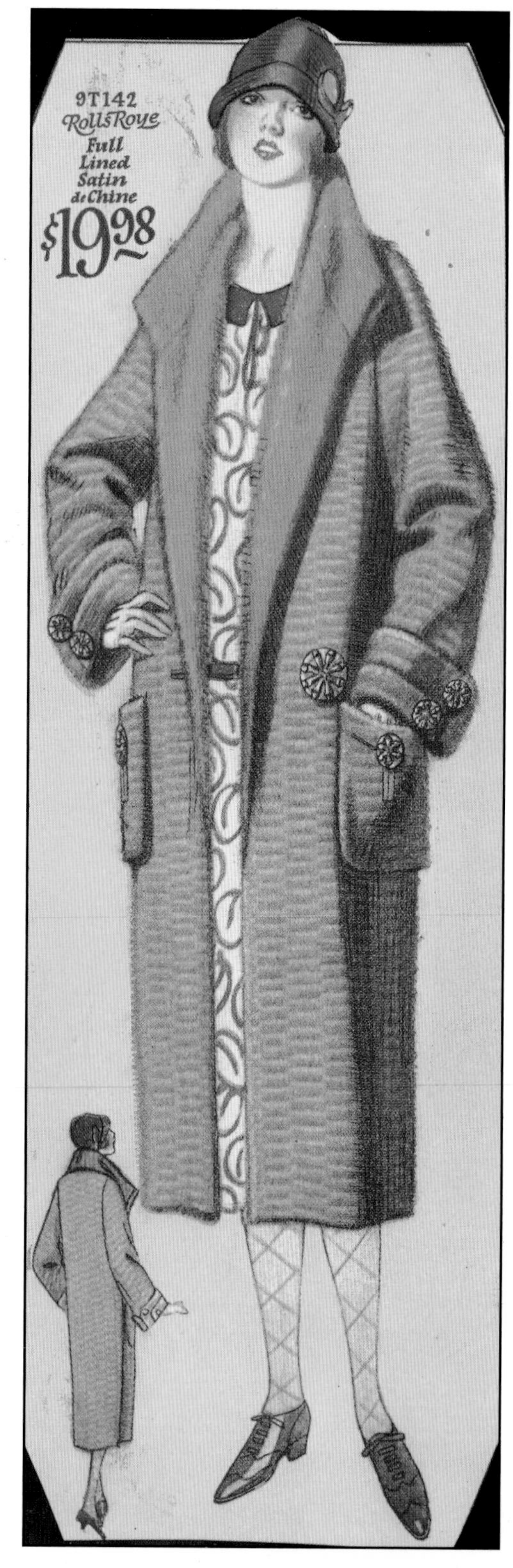

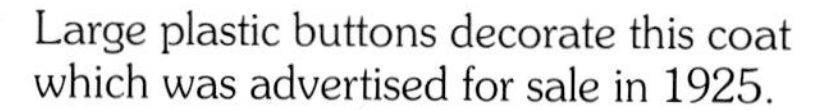

Large plastic buttons decorate this coat which was advertised for sale in 1925.

Deeply carved and graduated black vulcanite beads, 1880s. $200.

Celluloid

Initially, celluloid was viewed as a substitute for ivory, tortoiseshell and amber. Ironically, when celluloid first appeared on the market in the 19th century, it was rather expensive, not a cheap imitation. As the years went on, the price was lowered dramatically and by the 1920s, celluloid was dirt cheap. Because celluloid was highly flammable, it was eventually replaced with other products, even though cellulose nitrate was said to be the strongest thermoplastic with many advantages and desirable properties. Because of the many desirable characteristics of celluloid, fabrication became easy and endless items were continually being created. New experimentation was constantly being done, however, to find a less flammable substitute. As the years progressed, new plastics were developed that didn't pose a risk of bursting into flames.

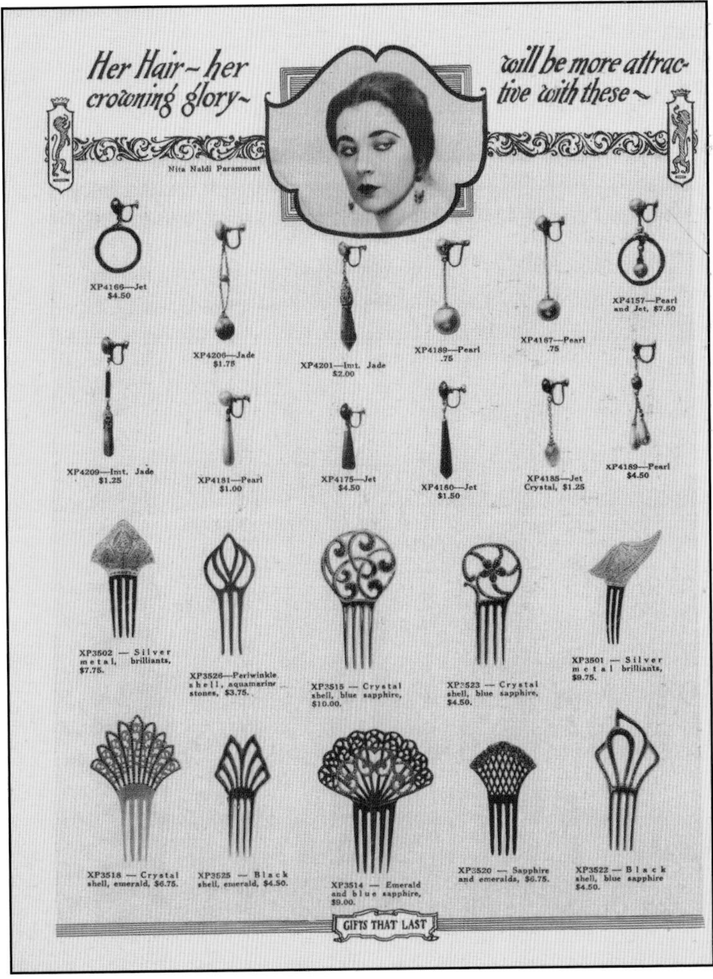

Jeweled celluloid hair combs advertised for sale in 1922 in the Blue Book Store Pictorial.

Inexpensive hair jewelry and combs made of celluloid and offered for sale in 1937.

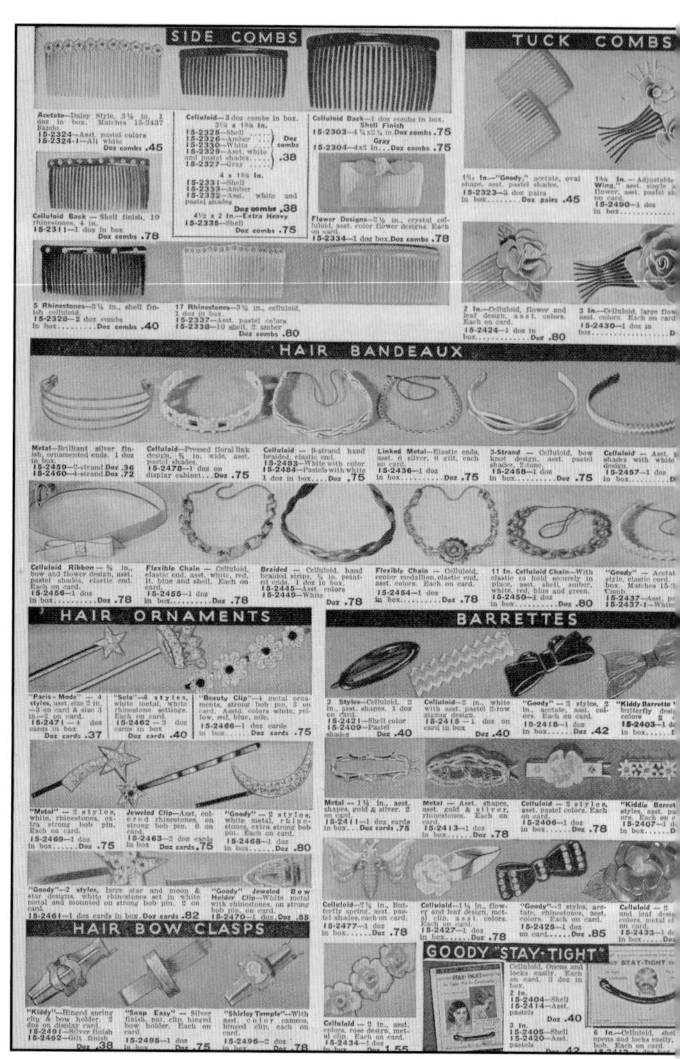

SIDE COMBS

Acetate—Daisy Style, 3½ in. 1 doz in box. Matches 15-2437 Bando.
15-2324—Asst. pastel colors
15-2324-1—All white
Doz combs .45

Celluloid—2 doz combs in box.
3¼ x 1¾ in.
15-2325—Shell
15-2326—Amber
15-2330—White
15-2329—Asst. white and pastel shades
15-2327—Gray
Doz combs .38
4 x 1¾ In.
15-2331—Shell
15-2333—Amber
15-2332—Asst. white and pastel shades
Doz combs .38
4½ x 2 In.—Extra Heavy
15-2335—Shell
Doz combs .75

Celluloid Back—1 doz combs in box.
Shell Finish
15-2303—4¼x2¼ in. Doz combs .75
Gray
15-2304—4x2 in... Doz combs .75

Celluloid Back — Shell finish, 10 rhinestones, 4 in.
15-2311—1 doz in box
Doz combs .78

Flower Designs—3½ in., crystal celluloid, asst. color flower designs. Each on card.
15-2334—1 doz box. Doz combs .78

5 Rhinestones—3¼ in., shell finish celluloid.
15-2328—2 doz combs in box......... Doz combs .40

17 Rhinestones—3½ in., celluloid, 1 doz in box.
15-2337—Asst. pastel colors
15-2338—10 shell, 2 amber
Doz combs .80

TUCK COMBS

1⅝ In.—"Goody," acetate, oval shape, asst. pastel shades.
15-2323—3 doz pairs in box........ Doz pairs .45

1¾ In. — Adjustable "Wing," asst. single flower, asst. pastel sh... on card.
15-2490—1 doz in box...........

2 In.—Celluloid, flower and leaf design, asst. colors. Each on card.
15-2424—1 doz in box............ Doz .80

3 In.—Celluloid, large flow... asst. colors. Each on card
15-2430—1 doz in box.................. D...

HAIR BANDEAUX

Metal—Brilliant silver finish, ornamented ends. 1 doz in box.
15-2459—2-strand Doz .36
15-2460—4-strand Doz .72

Celluloid—Pressed floral link design, ⅝ in. wide, asst. pastel shades.
15-2478—1 doz on display cabinet... Doz .75

Celluloid — 9-strand hand braided, elastic end.
15-2483—White with color
15-2484—Pastels with white
1 doz in box.... Doz .75

Linked Metal—Elastic ends, asst. 6 silver, 6 gilt, each on card.
15-2436—1 doz in box.......... Doz .75

3-Strand — Celluloid, bow knot design, asst. pastel shades, 2-tone.
15-2458—1 doz in box.......... Doz .75

Celluloid — Asst. ... shades with white design.
15-2457—1 doz in box.......... D...

Celluloid Ribbon — ⅝ in., bow and flower design, asst. pastel shades, elastic end. Each on card.
15-2456—1 doz in box.......... Doz .78

Flexible Chain — Celluloid, elastic end, asst. white, red, lt. blue and shell. Each on card.
15-2455—1 doz in box.......... Doz .78

Braided — Celluloid, hand braided strips, ½ in. pointed ends. 1 doz in box.
15-2445—Asst. colors
15-2449—White
Doz .78

Flexible Chain — Celluloid, center medallion, elastic end, asst. colors. Each on card.
15-2454—1 doz in box.......... Doz .78

11 In. Celluloid Chain—With elastic to hold securely in place, asst. shell, amber, white, red, blue and green.
15-2450—1 doz in box.......... Doz .80

"Goody" — Acetat... style, elastic cord... box. Matches 15-2... Comb.
15-2437—Asst. p...
15-2437-1—White

HAIR ORNAMENTS

"Paris-Mode" — 4 styles, asst. size 2 in. —3 on card & size 3 in.—2 on card.
15-2471—4 doz cards in box
Doz cards .37

"Solo"—6 styles, white metal, white rhinestone settings. Each on card.
15-2462—3 doz cards in box
Doz cards .40

"Beauty Clip"—4 metal ornaments, strong bob pin, 3 on card. Asstd. colors white, yellow, red, blue, nile.
15-2466—1 doz cards in box...... Doz cards .75

"Metal" — 2 styles, white, rhinestones, extra strong bob pin. Each on card.
15-2469—1 doz in box...... Doz .75

Jeweled Clip—Asst. colored rhinestones, on strong bob pin, 6 on card.
15-2463—2 doz cards in box Doz cards .75

"Goody" — 2 styles, white metal, rhinestones, extra strong bob pin. Each on card.
15-2468—1 doz in box...... Doz .80

"Goody"—2 styles, large star and moon & star designs, white rhinestones set in white metal and mounted on strong bob pin. 2 on card.
15-2461—1 doz cards in box. Doz cards .82

"Goody" Jeweled Bow Holder Clip—White metal with rhinestones, on strong bob pin, on card.
15-2470—1 doz. Doz .85

BARRETTES

3 Styles—Celluloid, 2 in., asst. shapes, 1 doz on card.
15-2421—Shell color
15-2409—Pastel shades Doz .40

Celluloid—2 in., white with asst. pastel 2-row zigzag design.
15-2415 — 1 doz on card in box
Doz .40

"Goody" — 2 styles, 2 in., acetate, asst. colors. Each on card.
15-2418—1 doz in box...... Doz .42

"Kiddy Barrette"... butterfly desi... colors...
15-2403—1 d... in box......

Metal — 1¼ in., asst. shapes, gold & silver. 2 on card.
15-2411—1 doz cards in box... Doz cards .75

Metal — Asst. shapes, asst. gold & silver, rhinestones. Each on card.
15-2413—1 doz in box...... Doz .78

Celluloid — 2 styles, asst. pastel colors. Each on card.
15-2406—1 doz in box...... Doz .78

"Kiddie Barret... styles, asst. pa... ors. Each on c...
15-2407—1 d... in box...... D...

Celluloid—2¼ in., Butterfly spring, asst. pastel shades, each on card.
15-2477—1 doz in box...... Doz .78

Celluloid—1¼ in., flower and leaf design, metal clip, asst. colors. Each on card.
15-2427—1 doz in box...... Doz .78

"Goody"—2 styles, acetate, rhinestones, asst. colors. Each on card.
15-2425—1 doz on card...... Doz .85

Celluloid — 2 ... and leaf desi... colors, metal cl... on card.
15-2433—1 d... in box...... Doz

HAIR BOW CLASPS

"Kiddy"—Hinged spring clip & bow holder. 2 doz on display card.
15-2491—Silver finish
15-2492—Gilt finish
Doz .38

"Snap Easy" — Silver finish, pat. clip, hinged bow holder. Each on card.
15-2495—1 doz in box...... Doz .75

"Shirley Temple"—With asst. color cameos, hinged clip, each on card.
15-2496—2 doz in box...... Doz .78

Celluloid — 2 in., asst. colors, rose design, metal clip. Each on card.
15-2434—1 doz in box...... Doz 1.55

GOODY "STAY-TIGHT"

Celluloid. Opens and locks easily. Each on card. 3 doz in box.
2 In.
15-2404—Shell
15-2414—Asst. pastels
Doz .40
3 In.
15-2405—Shell
15-2420—Asst. pastels
Doz .42

6 In.—Celluloid, shel... opens and locks easily, bob. Each on card.

Hair combs in a mixture of assorted sizes, shapes and colors made of celluloid with rhinestone accents; two were made with aluminum tops, 1920s. $125-$225 each.

Celluloid hair combs showing variations in color and design, 1920s. $150-$225 each.

Layered celluloid pendant stamped Arch Amerith. $95.

Cellulose Acetate

By 1894, a synthetic plastic made of cellulose acetate was the up-and-coming synthetic plastic. Around eight years later, it was being used in film for the photography industry and then, as a filler, woven into fabrics. By the 1940s, multi-strand faux pearl necklaces were designed with cores made of cellulose acetate. This allowed for larger beads and more strands and an overall much larger necklace. Large jewelry made fashion statements and these draped necklaces, as they were called, became an important part of the fashion scene for years. Many of the earlier simulated pearl necklaces had cores made of glass, which made the necklace much heavier and more expensive. Tell Manufacturing Company of Newark, New Jersey and Teckna Company of New York manufactured simulated pearls with acetate cores in the late 40s for Coro. Koppers Company, a plastics company in Pittsburgh, Pennsylvania, created cellulose acetate multi-strand faux pearl necklaces, which were advertised to *look like the real thing, warm to the touch, light in weight and practically unbreakable.* In the late 1930s, DuPont introduced a cellulose acetate plastic made of cotton linters and acetic acid and named it Plastacele which was used for costume jewelry. By the mid 20th century, cellulose acetate was the "most widely used of all thermoplastic molding materials" according to *Modern Plastics Encyclopedia.*

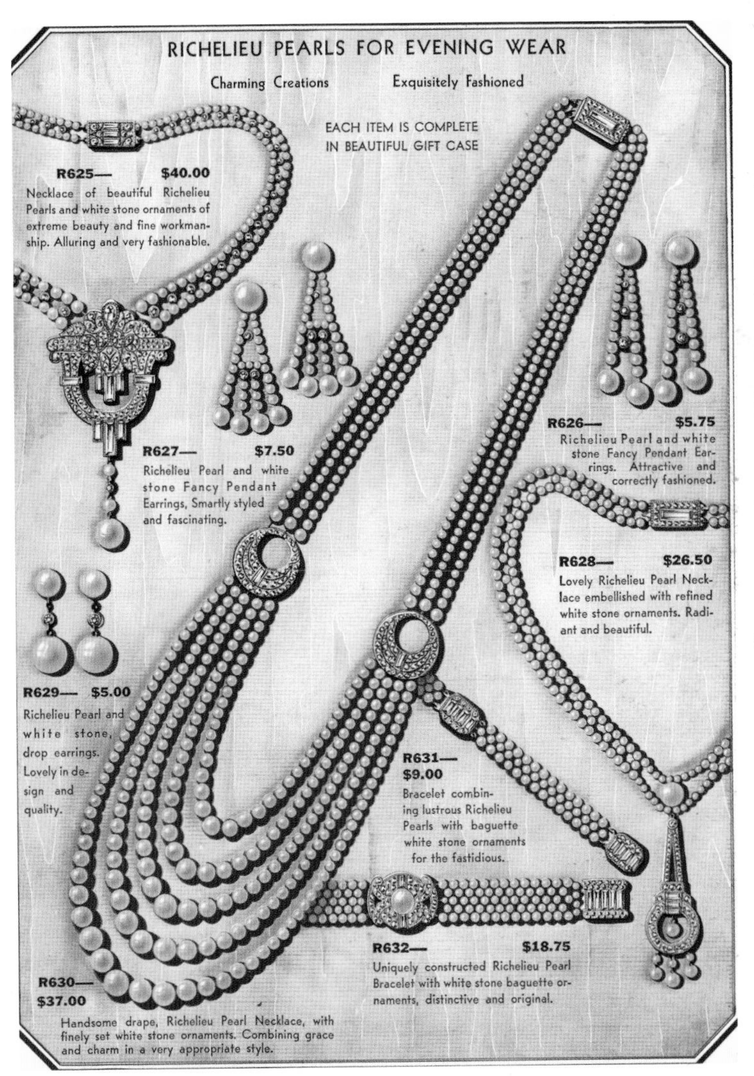

Cellulose acetate was being used in the first half of the 20th century for the manufacture of simulated pearls. These Richelieu pearls were designed for evening wear in 1931.

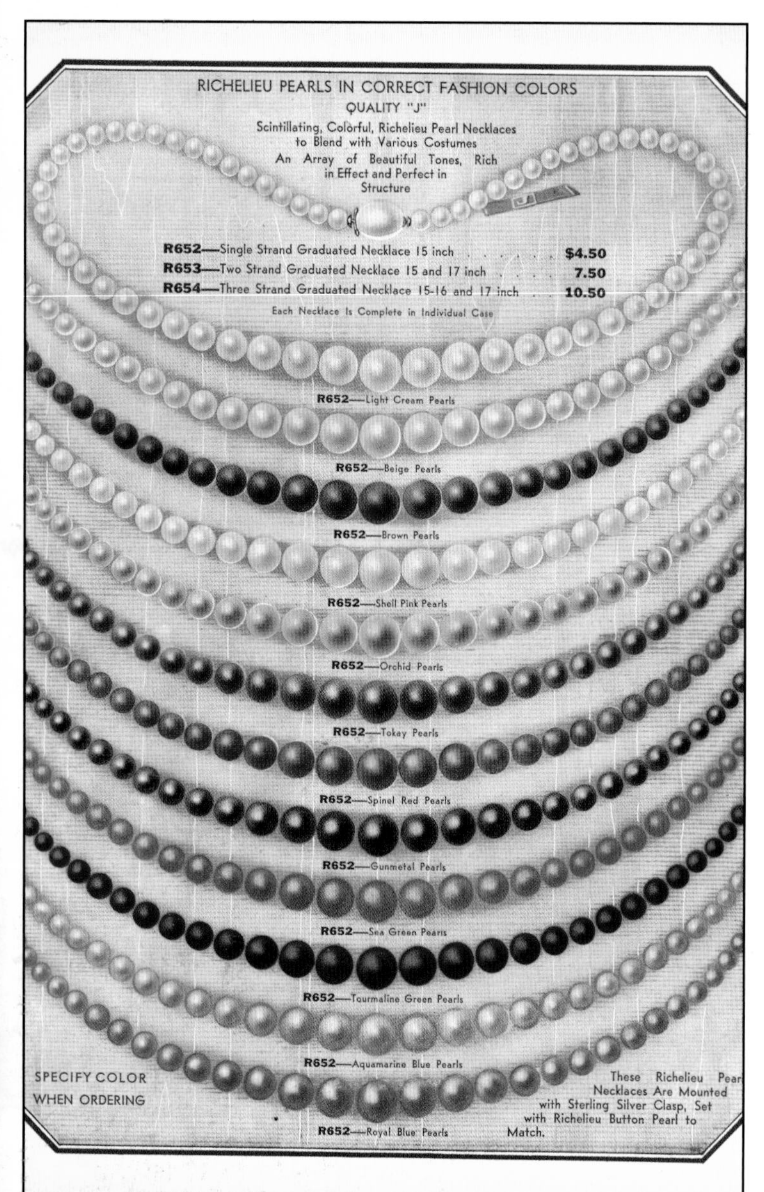

Assorted fashion colors and sizes of Richelieu imitation pearls offered for sale in the 1930s.

Simulated pearls with acetate cores manufactured by Tell Mfg. Co., Newark, New Jersey in 1949.

Bakelite

A patent for the first true synthetic plastic appeared in 1909. Belgium born Dr. Leo H. Baekeland accidentally invented a thermosetting phenol formaldehyde resin, which he later called Bakelite. After years of research and more patents, Baekeland became the president of The Bakelite Corporation. Later, as a unit of Union Carbide and Carbon Corporation, The Bakelite Corporation produced a host of phenolic molding plastics and cast resins that were widely used in the first half of the 20th century. Items such as handles on electrical appliances, cook pot handles, housings for business machines and even simulated stag handles for carving sets were made of Bakelite molding plastics. Bakelite phenolic molding plastics were heat-resistant, had great dimensional stability, wonderful insulating qualities and could be produced at a very low cost. Bakelite general-purpose cast resins could be produced in a wide palette of rich colors and could also be made clear, transparent, translucent and opaque. Two-toned or dual effects were also common. Many 1930s and 1940s bangle bracelets were made of this two-toned or marbled Bakelite. Much jewelry made during the Depression years was made of Bakelite cast resin. The main reason for its abundant use was cost. It was inexpensive to make and therefore the consumer during the hard times of the 1930s and early 1940s was able to afford it. This material was also lightweight allowing for large pieces to be fabricated from this material. Chunky bracelets, dress clips, brooches, belt buckles and huge necklaces were common. Bakelite cast resin also produced jewelry that remained warm when touched. Depression jewelry was designed with a touch of whimsy. Even though times were tough, this whimsical jewelry made people smile. Bakelite jewelry during this era was made in the form of common items like fruits, vegetables, puppy dogs, horses, airplanes, hearts, flowers, school tablets, pencils, flags and elephants among others. Wide bracelets were carved, reverse-carved and laminated. Colorful phenolic thermoset plastic jewelry dominated the fashion scene during the 1930s. In the Art Deco period of the 1930s, Bakelite was used in combination with chrome to create wonderful geometric designs in jewelry.

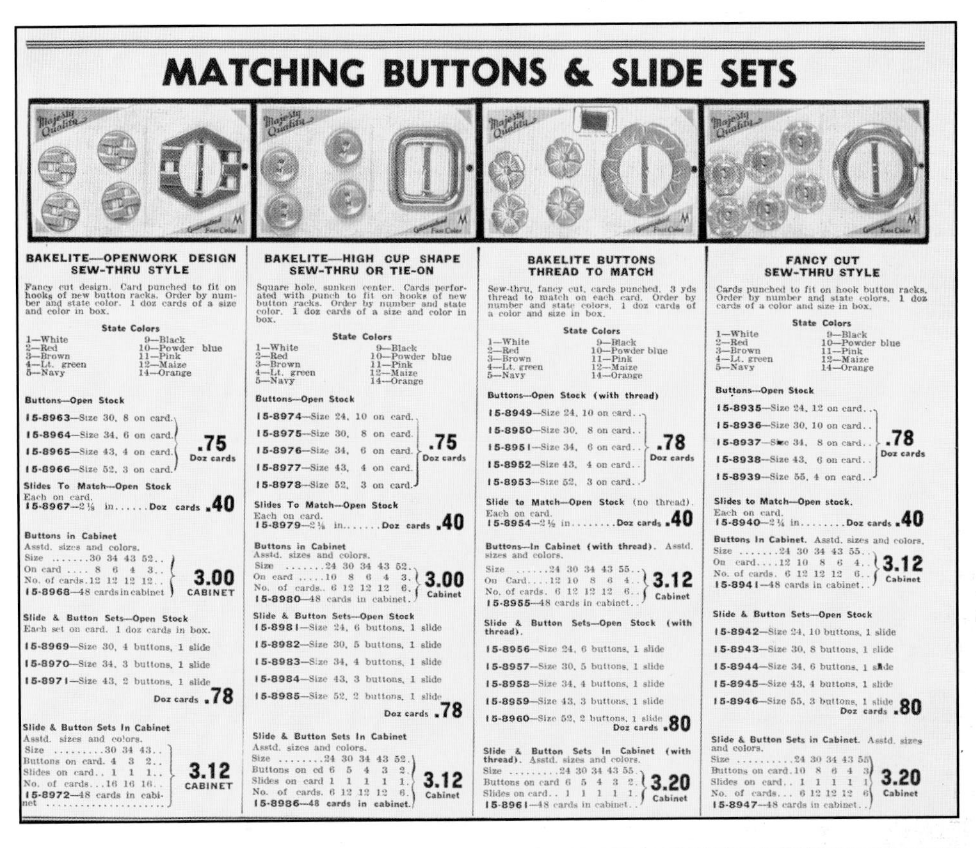

MATCHING BUTTONS & SLIDE SETS

BAKELITE—OPENWORK DESIGN SEW-THRU STYLE

Fancy cut design. Card punched to fit on hooks of new button racks. Order by number and state color. 1 doz cards of a size and color in box.

State Colors
1—White, 2—Red, 3—Brown, 4—Lt. green, 5—Navy, 9—Black, 10—Powder blue, 11—Pink, 12—Maize, 14—Orange

Buttons—Open Stock
15-8963—Size 30, 8 on card.
15-8964—Size 34, 6 on card.
15-8965—Size 43, 4 on card.
15-8966—Size 52, 3 on card.
.75 Doz cards

Slides To Match—Open Stock
Each on card.
15-8967—2⅛ in...... Doz cards .40

Buttons in Cabinet
Asstd. sizes and colors.
Size ....30 34 43 52..
On card .... 8 6 4 3..
No. of cards.12 12 12 12..
15-8968—48 cards in cabinet
3.00 CABINET

Slide & Button Sets—Open Stock
Each set on card. 1 doz cards in box.
15-8969—Size 30, 4 buttons, 1 slide
15-8970—Size 34, 3 buttons, 1 slide
15-8971—Size 43, 2 buttons, 1 slide
Doz cards .78

Slide & Button Sets In Cabinet
Asstd. sizes and colors.
Size ....30 34 43..
Buttons on card. 4 3 2..
Slides on card.. 1 1 1..
No. of cards...16 16 16..
15-8972—48 cards in cabinet ....
3.12 CABINET

BAKELITE—HIGH CUP SHAPE SEW-THRU OR TIE-ON

Square hole, sunken center. Cards perforated with punch to fit on hooks of new button racks. Order by number and state color. 1 doz cards of a size and color in box.

State Colors
1—White, 2—Red, 3—Brown, 4—Lt. green, 5—Navy, 9—Black, 10—Powder blue, 11—Pink, 12—Maize, 14—Orange

Buttons—Open Stock
15-8974—Size 24, 10 on card.
15-8975—Size 30, 8 on card.
15-8976—Size 34, 6 on card.
15-8977—Size 43, 4 on card.
15-8978—Size 52, 3 on card.
.75 Doz cards

Slides To Match—Open Stock
Each on card.
15-8979—2⅛ in....... Doz cards .40

Buttons in Cabinet
Asstd. sizes and colors.
Size ....24 30 34 43 52.
On card .....10 8 6 4 3.
No. of cards.. 6 12 12 12 6.
15-8980—48 cards in cabinet.
3.00 Cabinet

Slide & Button Sets—Open Stock
15-8981—Size 24, 6 buttons, 1 slide
15-8982—Size 30, 5 buttons, 1 slide
15-8983—Size 34, 4 buttons, 1 slide
15-8984—Size 43, 3 buttons, 1 slide
15-8985—Size 52, 2 buttons, 1 slide
Doz cards .78

Slide & Button Sets In Cabinet
Asstd. sizes and colors.
Size ....24 30 34 43 52.
Buttons on cd 6 5 4 3 2.
Slides on card 1 1 1 1 1.
No. of cards. 6 12 12 12 6.
15-8986—48 cards in cabinet.
3.12 Cabinet

BAKELITE BUTTONS THREAD TO MATCH

Sew-thru, fancy cut, cards punched. 3 yds thread to match on each card. Order by number and state colors. 1 doz cards of a color and size in box.

State Colors
1—White, 2—Red, 3—Brown, 4—Lt. green, 5—Navy, 9—Black, 10—Powder blue, 11—Pink, 12—Maize, 14—Orange

Buttons—Open Stock (with thread)
15-8949—Size 24, 10 on card..
15-8950—Size 30, 8 on card..
15-8951—Size 34, 6 on card..
15-8952—Size 43, 4 on card..
15-8953—Size 52, 3 on card..
.78 Doz cards

Slide to Match—Open Stock (no thread). Each on card.
15-8954—2½ in........ Doz cards .40

Buttons—In Cabinet (with thread). Asstd. sizes and colors.
Size ......24 30 34 43 55..
On Card....12 10 8 6 4..
No. of cards. 6 12 12 12 6..
15-8955—48 cards in cabinet..
3.12 Cabinet

Slide & Button Sets—Open Stock (with thread).
15-8956—Size 24, 6 buttons, 1 slide
15-8957—Size 30, 5 buttons, 1 slide
15-8958—Size 34, 4 buttons, 1 slide
15-8959—Size 43, 3 buttons, 1 slide
15-8960—Size 52, 2 buttons, 1 slide
Doz cards .80

Slide & Button Sets In Cabinet (with thread). Asstd. sizes and colors.
Size ....24 30 34 43 55.
Buttons on card 6 5 4 3 2.
Slides on card.. 1 1 1 1 1.
15-8961—48 cards in cabinet..
3.20 Cabinet

FANCY CUT SEW-THRU STYLE

Cards punched to fit on hook button racks. Order by number and state colors. 1 doz cards of a color and size in box.

State Colors
1—White, 2—Red, 3—Brown, 4—Lt. green, 5—Navy, 9—Black, 10—Powder blue, 11—Pink, 12—Maize, 14—Orange

Buttons—Open Stock
15-8935—Size 24, 12 on card..
15-8936—Size 30, 10 on card..
15-8937—Size 34, 8 on card..
15-8938—Size 43, 6 on card..
15-8939—Size 55, 4 on card..
.78 Doz cards

Slides to Match—Open stock.
Each on card.
15-8940—2¼ in........ Doz cards .40

Buttons In Cabinet. Asstd. sizes and colors.
Size ....24 30 34 43 55..
On card....12 10 8 6 4..
No. of cards. 6 12 12 12 6..
15-8941—48 cards in cabinet..
3.12 Cabinet

Slide & Button Sets—Open Stock
15-8942—Size 24, 10 buttons, 1 slide
15-8943—Size 30, 8 buttons, 1 slide
15-8944—Size 34, 6 buttons, 1 slide
15-8945—Size 43, 4 buttons, 1 slide
15-8946—Size 55, 3 buttons, 1 slide
Doz cards .80

Slide & Button Sets in Cabinet. Asstd. sizes and colors.
Size 24 30 34 43 55
Buttons on card.10 8 6 4 3
Slides on card.. 1 1 1 1 1
No. of cards... 6 12 12 12 6
15-8947—48 cards in cabinet..
3.20 Cabinet

Matching buttons and slide sets made of Bakelite in 1937.

Assortment of cloak clasps, buckles and buttons made of Bakelite and embellished with metal accents, stones or carvings, early 20th century. $35-$95 each.

Two necklaces, rectangular cameo brooch, Bakelite, 1920s. $195-$295 each.

Two green Bakelite dress clips with varied ornamentation, 1930s. $125 each.

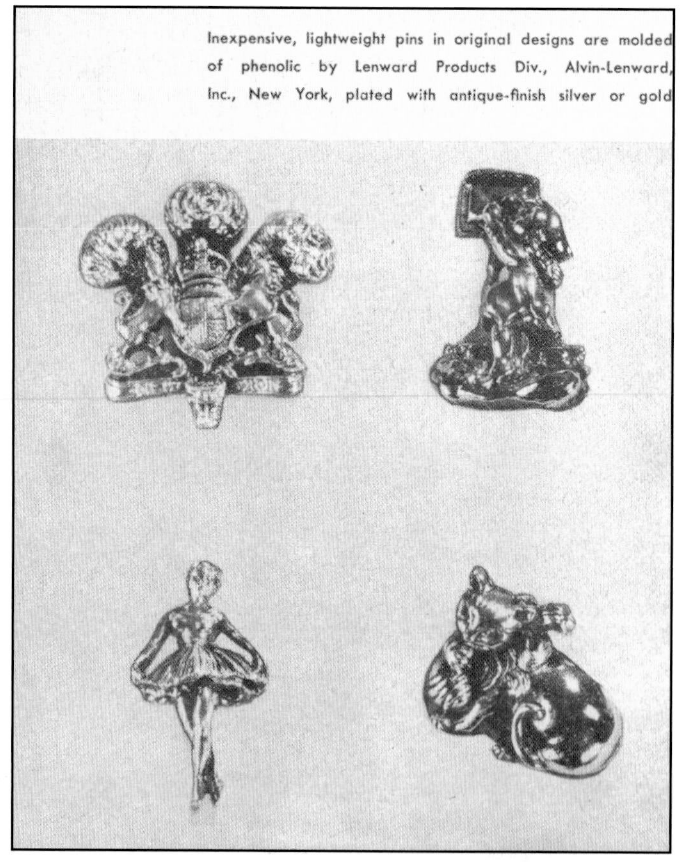

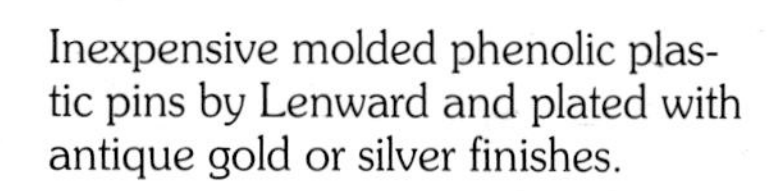

Inexpensive molded phenolic plastic pins by Lenward and plated with antique gold or silver finishes.

Galalith

Galalith was the trade name used to describe basically the same type of material. These pieces are extremely collectible today. By the 1940s, necklace and earring sets made with strands of cast phenolic beads in shades of amber and tortoiseshell were produced for Castlecliff by Mastercraft Plastics Company. This jewelry was inexpensive and allowed the average working class to afford the luxury of owning costume jewelry.

Galalith bracelets offered for sale in 1925 from the National Cloak and Suit Company.

Art Deco Egyptian Revival, Galalith, brass and molded glass, 1920s. $85-$195 each.

Catalin

Many other companies produced similar phenolic plastics and marketed them under different trade names. Catalin was one of the most popular as well as Marblette and Prystal which was a clear phenolic plastic. The clear, as well as some of the colored Bakelite pieces oxidized over time and produced color changes. The most common was the clear which eventually changed to what we know today as *apple juice* Bakelite. Color stability was good with most colors except for light red, blue and green. Sometimes color can be restored to an older piece of Bakelite by re-polishing or re-buffing.

Beautiful fashions offered from Sears in 1938. Notice the model on the left wearing a chunky plastic flower bracelet and matching hair jewelry.

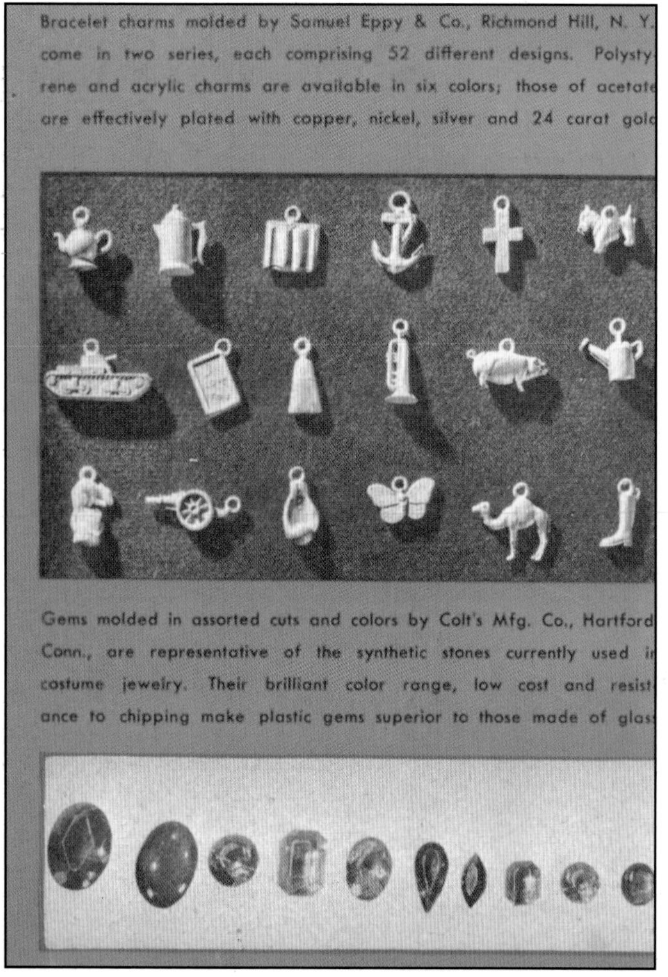

Bracelet charms molded by Samuel Eppy & Co., Richmond Hill, N. Y. come in two series, each comprising 52 different designs. Polysty-rene and acrylic charms are available in six colors; those of acetat are effectively plated with copper, nickel, silver and 24 carat gol

Gems molded in assorted cuts and colors by Colt's Mfg. Co., Hartford Conn., are representative of the synthetic stones currently used i costume jewelry. Their brilliant color range, low cost and resist ance to chipping make plastic gems superior to those made of glas

Two Bakelite buckles with applied metal decorations and rhinestone accents, 1930s. $95 each.

Molded plastic bracelet charms by Samuel Eppy & Company were available in polystyrene and acrylic. There were 52 different designs and 6 different colors. Charms made of acetate were plated in copper, nickel, silver or gold. Molded plastic gemstones were also available in many different colors, shapes and sizes and set into necklaces, earrings, brooches and bracelets.

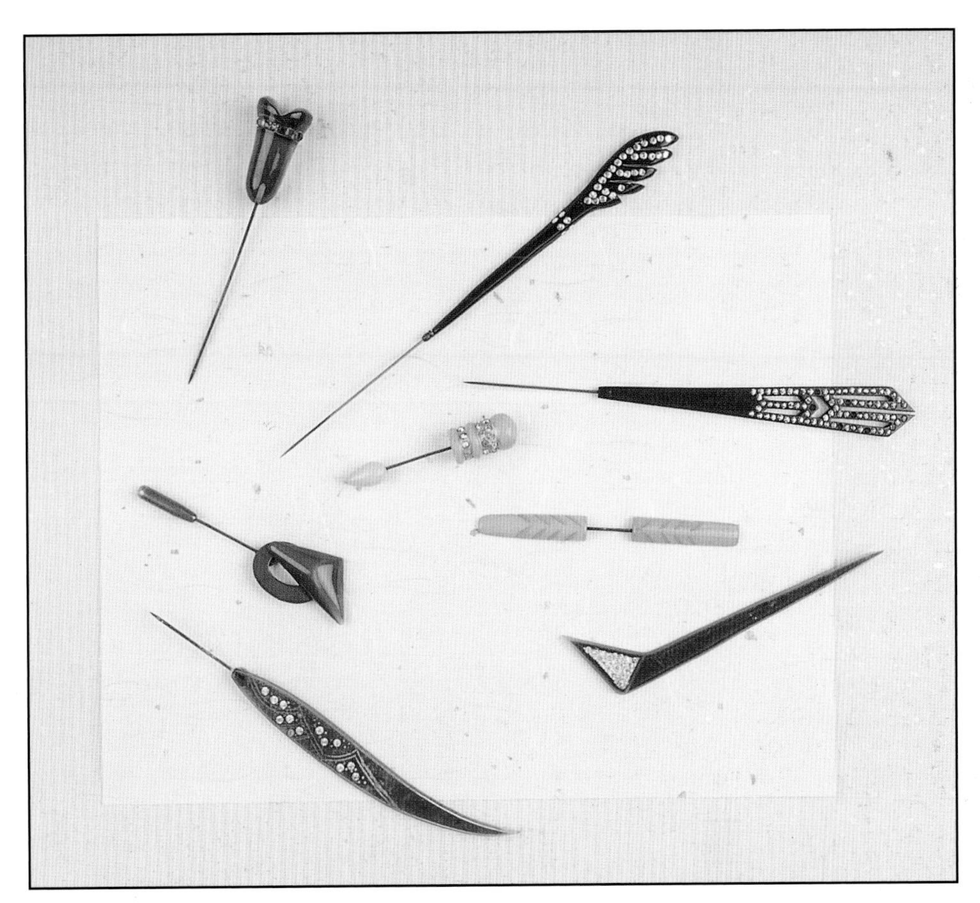

Assorted hat ornaments made of celluloid, Bakelite and Lucite and embellished with rhinestones, 1920s and 1930s. $50-$95 each.

Rhinestone-set hat ornaments and pins made of celluloid and other thermoplastics, 1920s and 1930s. $35-$75 each.

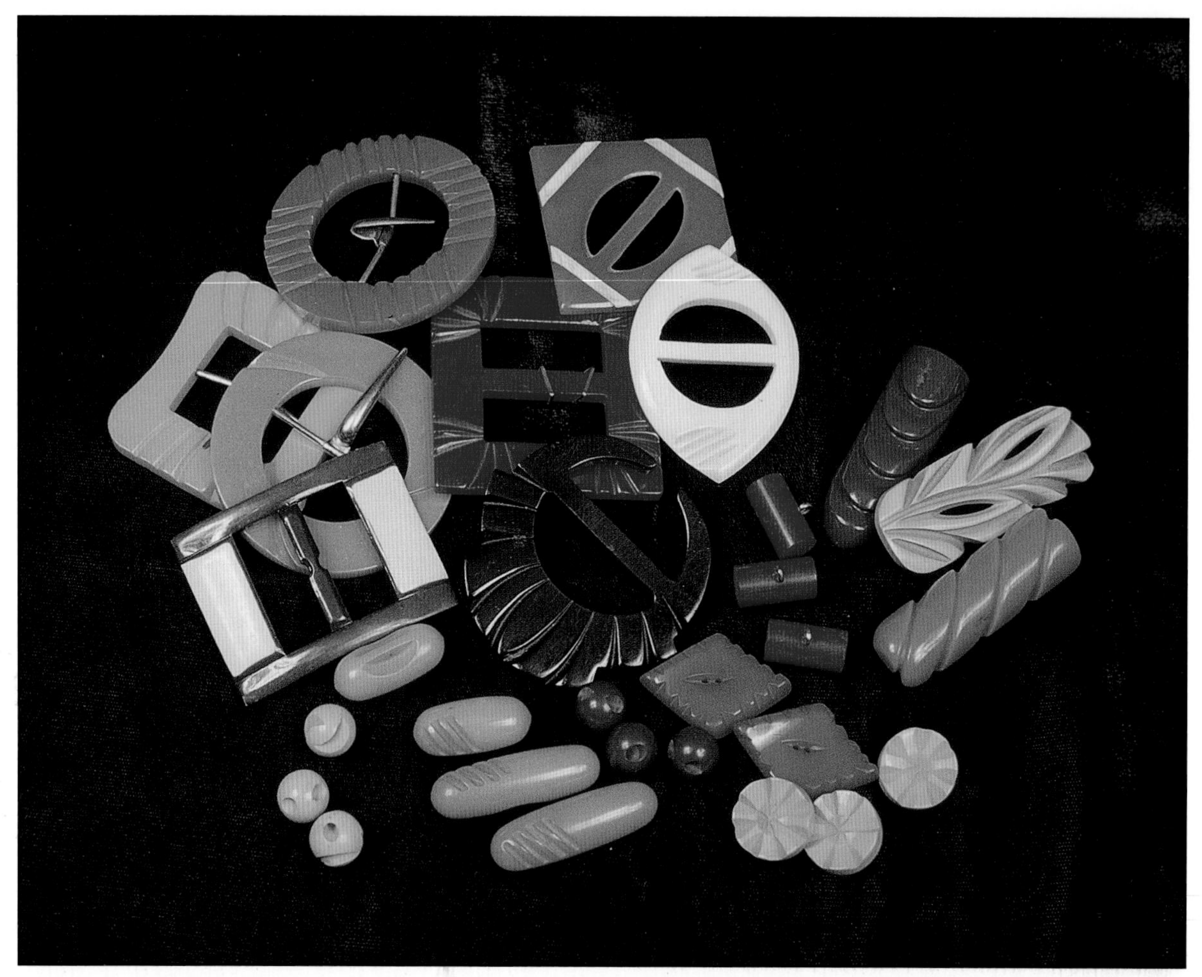

Buckles, buttons and clips made of Bakelite in the 1930s. $5-$50 each.

Art Deco clip, Bakelite with rhinestones, 1930. $125.

Matched pair of Art Deco brooches made of Bakelite with rhinestone accents. $145 pair.

Art Deco celluloid bangle bracelets cleverly set with clear and colored rhinestones. $100-$225 each.

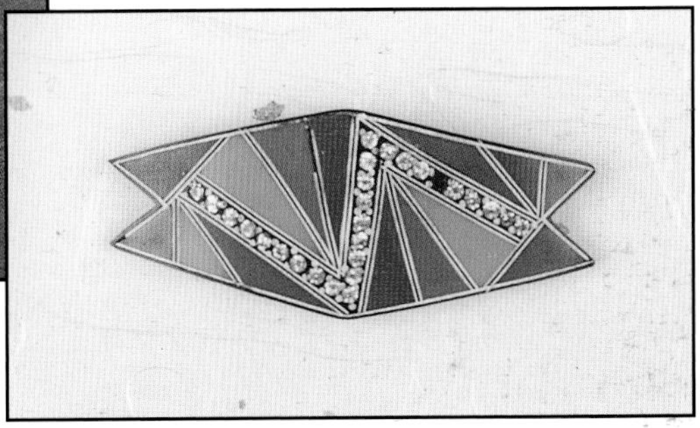

Multi-color Art Deco brooch made of thermoplastic and accented with rhinestones. $95.

Two Bakelite brooches with horse motifs under glass. $225 each.

Two bow designs in thermoplastic; one set with rhinestones. $85 each.

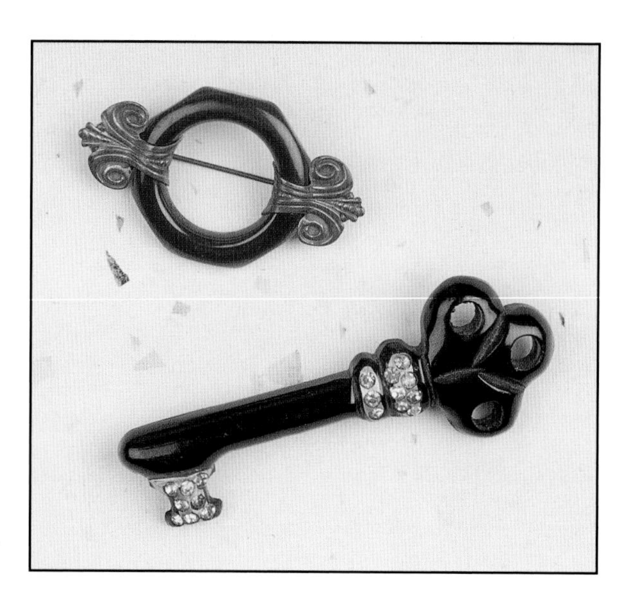

Thermoset plastic brooches designed with metal and rhinestone accents. $85 each.

Art Deco reverse-carved pendant necklace, apple juice Bakelite with rhinestones, celluloid link chain. $325.

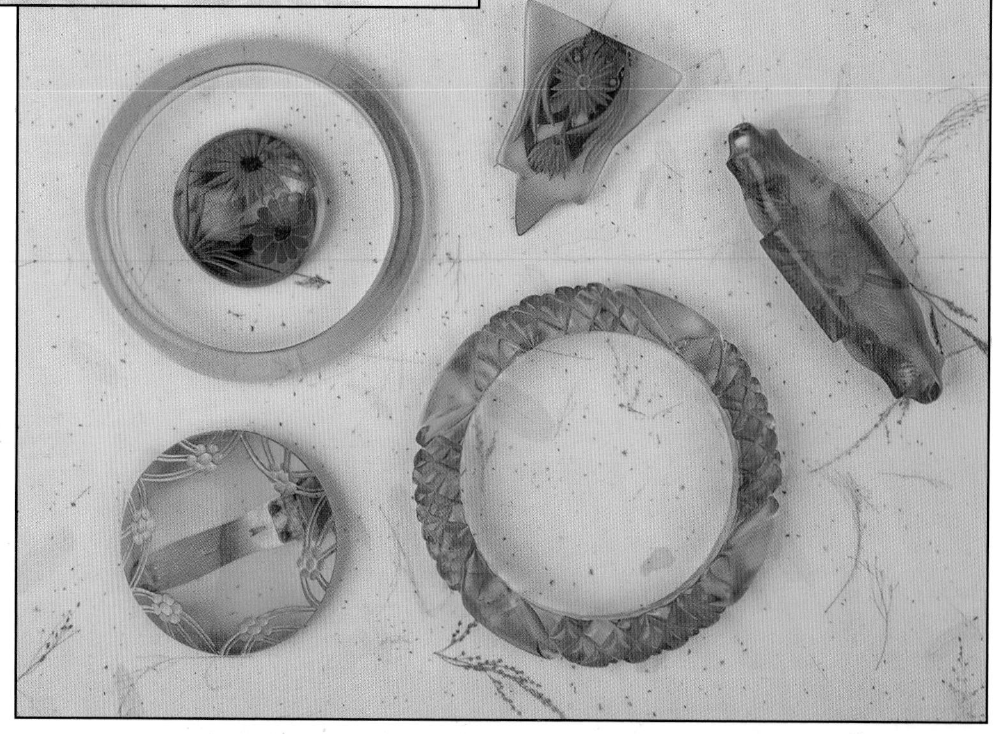

Smooth and carved bangle bracelets and reverse-carved clips and brooch, apple juice Bakelite. $195-345 each.

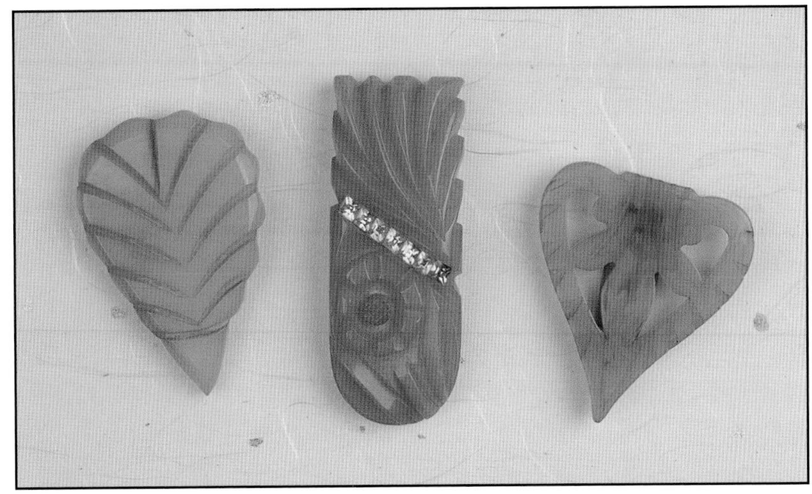

Dress clips, carved and embellished with rhinestones, butterscotch Bakelite. $175-225 each.

Bakelite bracelets, smooth and carved. $125-195 each.

Art Deco celluloid brooch, embellished with rhinestones. $175.

Pair of matched pins, molded plastic accented with colored rhinestones. $95 set.

Oval scenic brooch, laminated Pyralin. $125.

Flower petals of celluloid form hatpins embellished with rhinestones. $125 pair.

Cameo pendants and earrings made of Lucite and Bakelite with metal and Celluloid link chains. Pendants $100 each. Earrings $45.

Cameo pendant made of Lucite and Bakelite suspended from silk cord. $125.

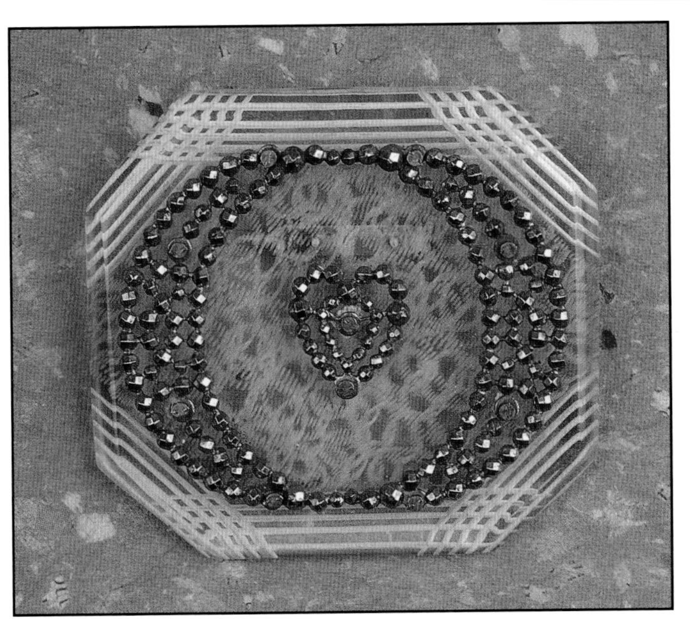

Reverse-carved Lucite brooch with cut steel decoration. $145.

Nosegay holder, Bakelite. $175.

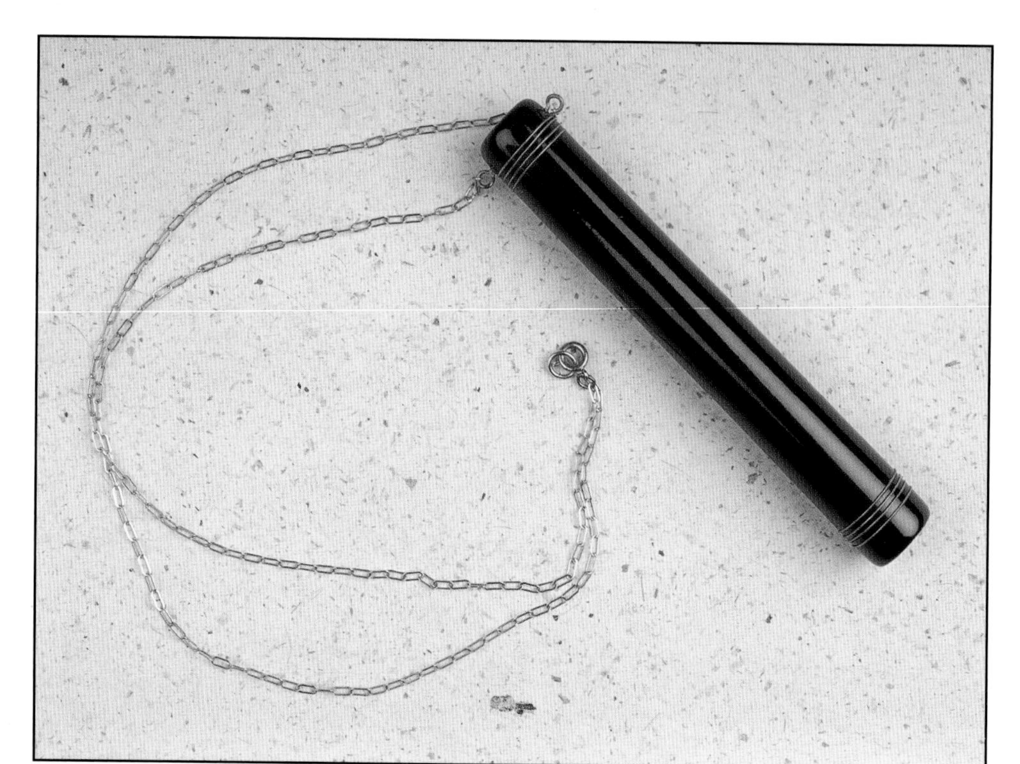

Bracelets, assorted plastics, early 20th century. $125-495 each.

Two initial pins made of plastic; one from the 30s and the other from the 70s. Can you tell which is which? $25-40 each.

Deeply carved clamper bracelet with floral designs, Bakelite. $495.

Solid green and marbled bangle bracelets, Bakelite. $100-195 each.

Black and butterscotch bangle bracelets, Bakelite. $145-195 each.

Chocolate brown bangles, carved Bakelite. $145-225 each.

Wide clamper bracelet and matching earrings, wood and Bakelite. $495 set.

Leaf, poinsettia and acorn brooches, wood and Bakelite. $245-325 each.

Necklace, wood and Bakelite beads. $245.

Brooch and matching screw-back earrings, carved Bakelite. $165 set.

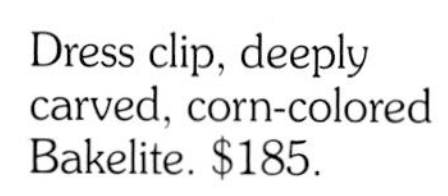

Dress clip, deeply carved, corn-colored Bakelite. $185.

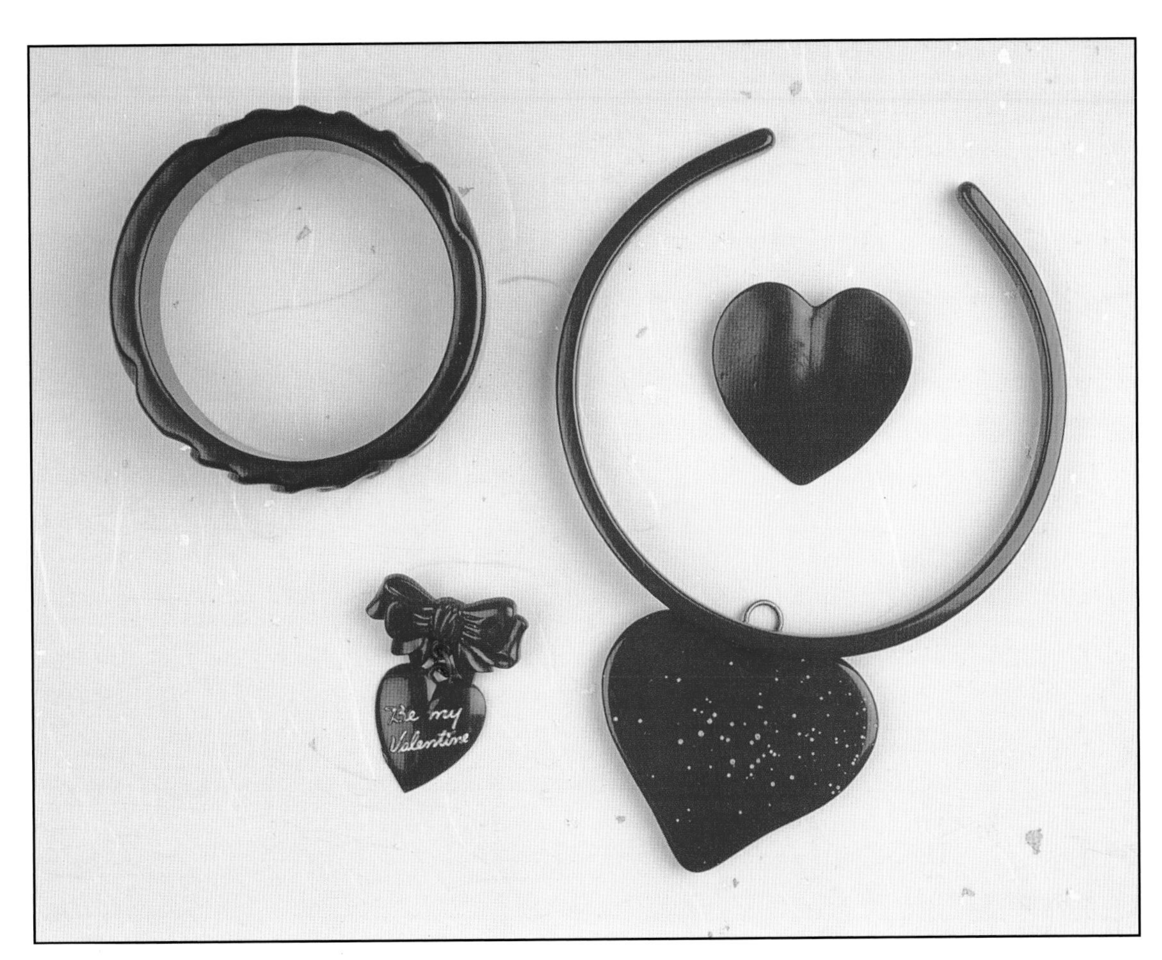

Bangle bracelet and choker made of Bakelite; thermoset heart brooches. $75-295 each.

Bead necklace, graduated and faceted Bakelite. $245.

Dress clip, brooch and earrings, Bakelite with metal accents. $75-195 each.

Thermoset plastic brooches made to resemble carved Bakelite. $45-125 each.

Large buckle, black Bakelite accented with carved corn Bakelite. $175.

Art Deco link bracelet, red Bakelite with chrome accents. $350.

Link bracelet, carved Bakelite. $275.

Carved buckles, corn and black Bakelite. $80-130 each.

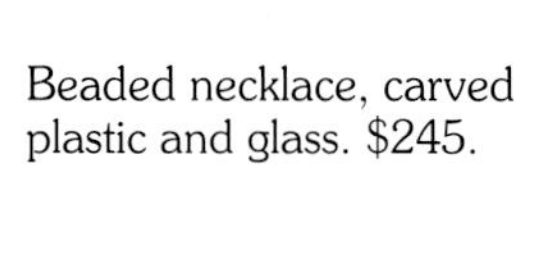

Beaded necklace, carved plastic and glass. $245.

Geometric shapes of corn and brown Bakelite make up this Art Deco demi-parure. $225 set.

Long beaded necklace, Bakelite. $275.

Intricately carved plastic bead necklaces; one with matching earrings. Necklaces $95 each; earrings $30.

Carved and molded plastic bead necklaces from the 1930s. The carved necklaces are also painted in pretty colors. $95 each.

Carved and graduated plastic bead necklaces; the beads are also painted. $95 each.

Carved bead necklaces, Bakelite and thermoset plastic. $95-125 each.

Two necklaces, celluloid flowers and celluloid chains. $135 each.

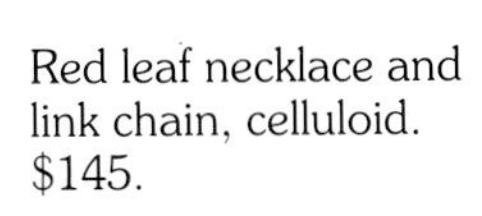

Red leaf necklace and link chain, celluloid. $145.

Baby blue celluloid leaf necklace with celluloid leaf chain. $165.

Pastel pink celluloid leaf necklace and bracelet demi-parure. $225 set.

Pretty pink flower necklace, green leaves, link chain, celluloid. $145.

Daisy necklace, filigree petals and leaves, link chain, celluloid. $175.

Openwork flowers, molded leaves and link chain make up this brilliant red demi-parure made of celluloid. $245 set.

Leaf necklace, celluloid. $95.

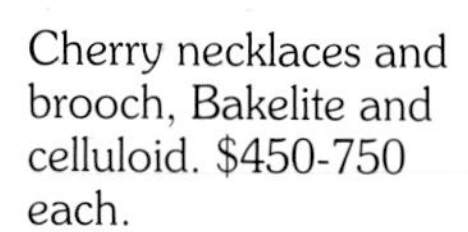

Cherry necklaces and brooch, Bakelite and celluloid. $450-750 each.

Necklace, brass and plastic. $135.

Heart necklace, thermoset plastic and celluloid. $135.

Art Deco neckpiece, chrome and Galalith. $395.

Fringed necklace, Bakelite, celluloid and glass. $275.

Art Deco necklace, root beer and apple juice Bakelite. $295.

Fringed necklace, celluloid and thermoset plastic. $145.

Thermoset plastic flower brooch in coral and green. $125.

Thermoset plastic flower bud necklace and bracelet strung on elastic. $150 set.

Pink thermoset plastic flower buds were string on elastic to make this adorable bracelet from the 1930s. $45.

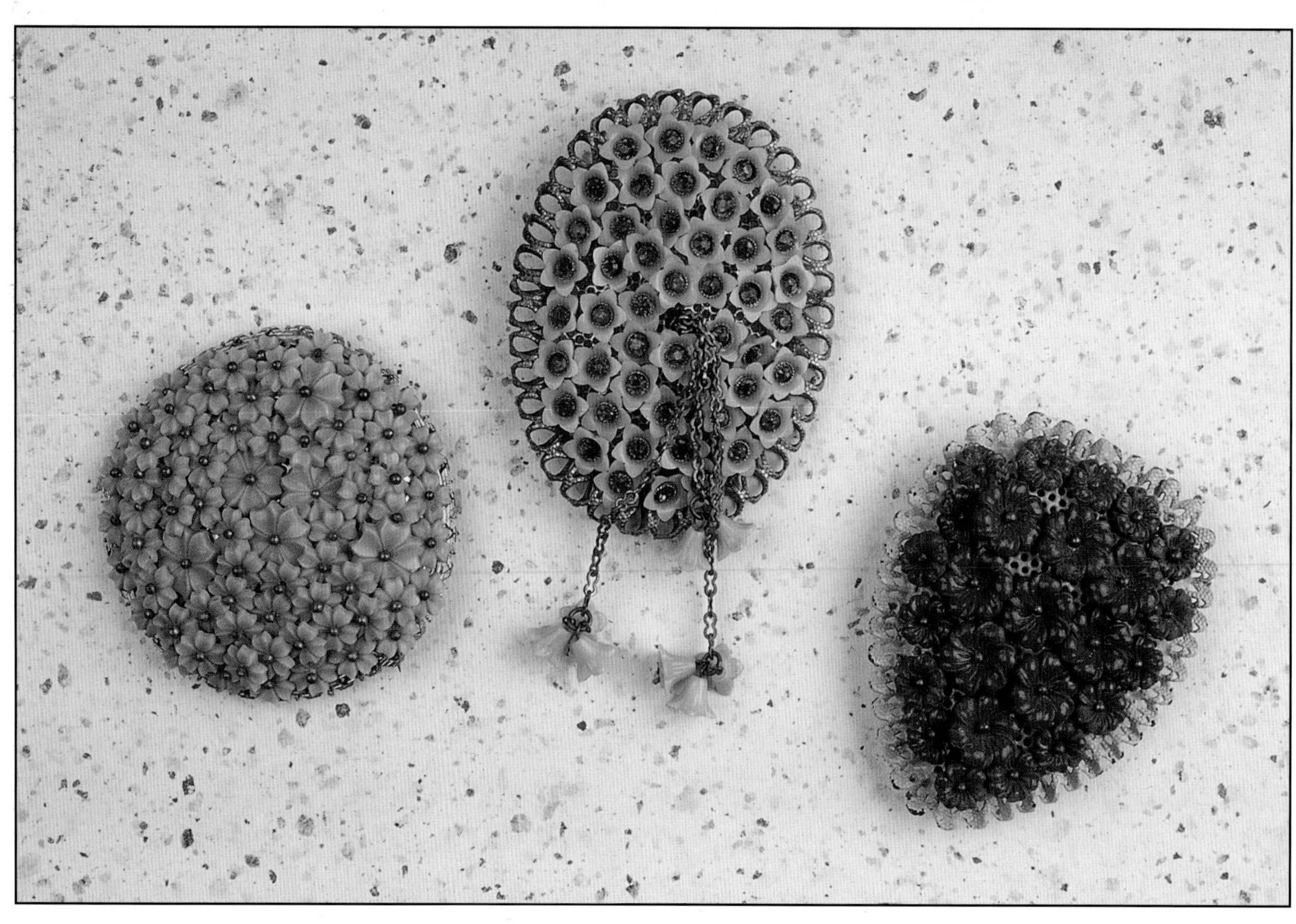

Similar in construction to early unsigned Haskell jewelry, these lovely brooches and dress clip were designed with tiny plastic flowers hand wired to brass filigree backgrounds. $145-195 each.

Necklace and brooch made of multi-colored plastic floral rosettes hand wired on brass. $185 set.

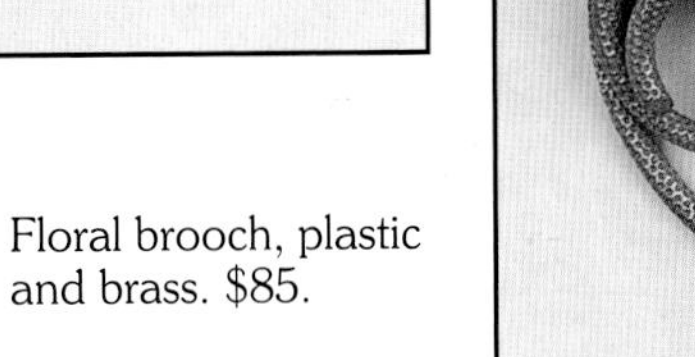

Floral brooch, plastic and brass. $85.

Brooch, hard plastic buttons and brass beads hand sewn on plastic backing. This is a perfect example of jewelry designed during the Depression era. Everyday articles, like buttons, were transformed into jewelry. $135.

Brooch, thermoset plastic flower buds on metal; flower earrings, celluloid. $48-65 each.

Screw-back earrings, twisted celluloid. $38.

Flower basket brooch and floral earrings, celluloid. $35-85 each.

Thermoset plastic floral brooch with dangles. $65.

Pair of dress clips, molded plastic and brass. $85 pair.

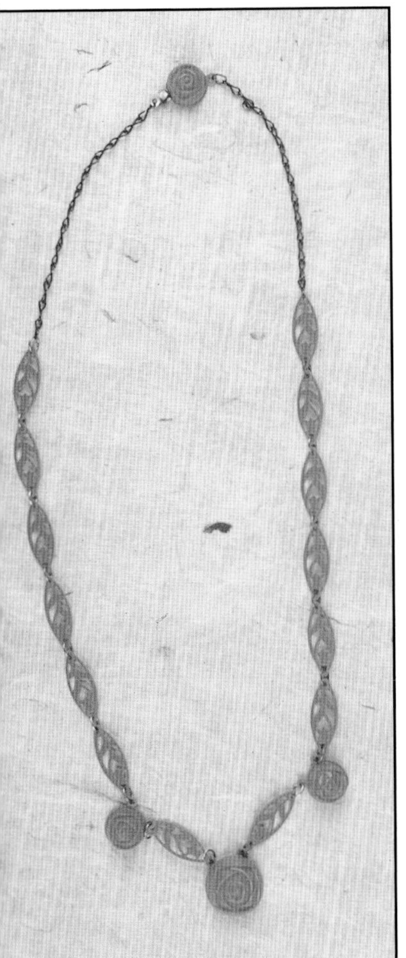

Coral-colored celluloid flower necklace with celluloid links. $125.

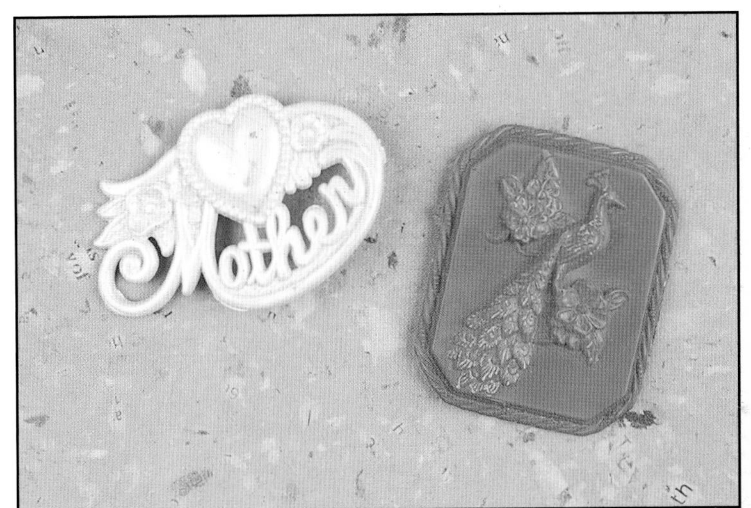

Thermoset plastic brooches. $48 each.

Link belt with flower buckle, celluloid. $145.

Articulated figural sailor brooch, He's a little upset that his pinback is showing. Bakelite. $500.

Four articulated plastic figural pins. $250 each.

Indian head pin with feather, celluloid and plastic. $95.

Large heart and arrow brooch, Bakelite. $500.

Figural brooch, celluloid, Made in Czechoslovakia. $135.

Bird on musical note novelty brooch, celluloid. $85.

Novelty brooch, "Huba Huba", thermoplastic. $85.

Hand brooch, painted fingernails, metal bracelet, Bakelite. $750.

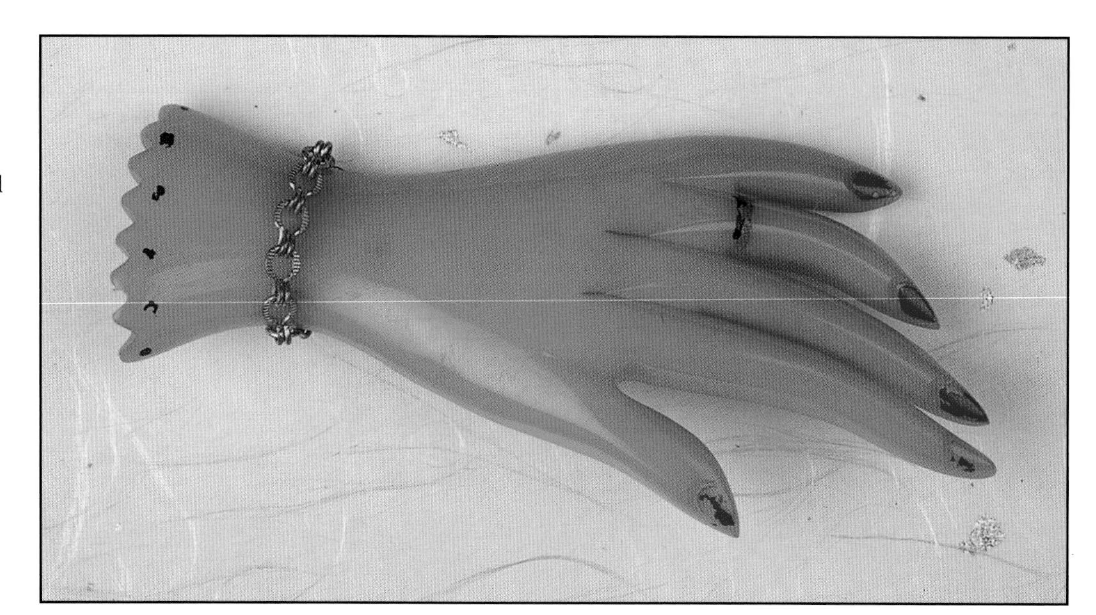

Bird brooch, cream corn colored Bakelite. $395.

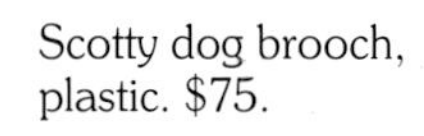

Scotty dog brooch, plastic. $75.

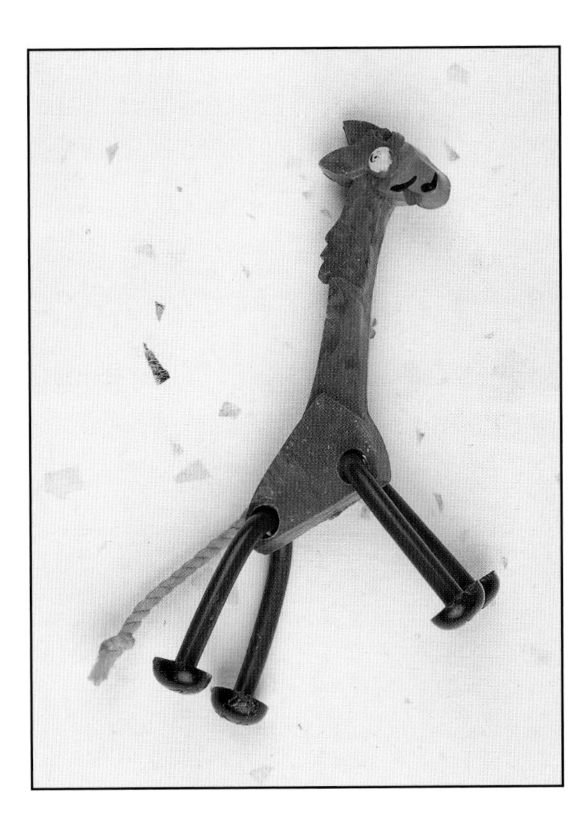

Giraffe brooch, movable legs, rope tail, plastic. $48.

High school pennant and megaphone, plastic and metal. $45.

Butterfly brooch and earring set, hand-painted plastic. $135 set.

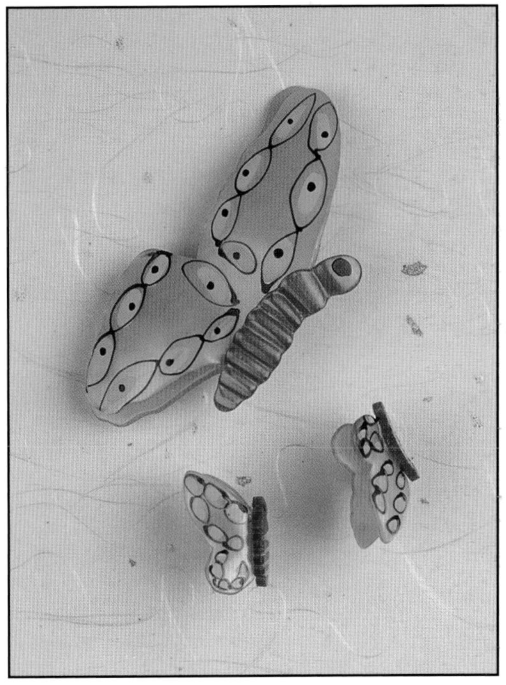

Novelty fruit and bug brooches, celluloid and plastic. $75 each.

Strawberry brooch,
hand-painted Bakelite.
$350.

Novelty dog, flamingo and palm tree brooches, thermoset plastic. $75-95 each.

Horse and fish brooches, wood and reverse-carved Lucite. $200 each.

Musical string instrument brooch, reverse-carved Lucite and Bakelite. $250.

Layered brooch, three-dimensional effect, plastic. $65.

Chapter 2

Mid-Century Modern

Lumarith

In 1937, the Celluloid Corporation created a new plastic used for jewelry manufacture and other items which was called Lumarith, a *new era plastic*. Popularity for this new synthetic polymer grew because it could be made in many different colors, like red, blue and violet. Within those colors it could be made transparent, translucent, mottled and variegated. It was also advertised as *odorless, tasteless and non-inflammable.* Lumarith was used in injection molding when manufactured in granule or powder form as well as sheets, rods and tubes for cutting and carving. Infinite variety became possible.

Even though this was an ad for an Orlon sweater, this 1950s model is wearing two blue plastic necklaces twisted at the wrist to look like bracelets. She is also wearing blue plastic earrings.

Model wearing red plastic beads, tortoise plastic sunglasses, plastic buttons on vest and faux leopard and black plastic handbag. Plastic was everywhere in the mid-1950s.

Metal Finishes

During the 1940s, most metals were in short supply because they were needed for the war effort. Sterling silver was still used for jewelry manufacture. Plastics filled the void and tremendous quantities of inexpensive jewelry were produced. Lightweight molded phenolic plastic figural pins, sprays, earrings and charms were popular and plated with gold or silver finishes. This plastic jewelry was advertised as the type to return a profit and not just sit on the shelf. They created an expensive look at a fraction of the cost.

Gold-plated cellulose acetate jewelry by Nina Wolf won the American Fashion Critics Award in 1946. This award was sponsored by Coty cosmetics company.

Richelieu Iridelle translucent pearl jewelry was extremely popular in the late 1940s. Its rainbow of colors was advertised as Beautiful as a sunset…just as elusive. Single and double strand necklaces, earrings, bracelets, brooches and rings were offered.

Jewel encrusted plastic fruit pin, metal leaves. $150.

Richelieu IRIDELLE plastic beads popular in 1946. $20-95 each.

Charms

Plastic charms made for bracelets were molded by Samuel Eppy & Co. and they were available in two different series with 52 different designs in each. Acrylic and polystyrene charms were available in assorted colors while acetate charms were plated with silver, nickel, copper and gold.

Polystyrene

Another low cost plastic was polystyrene. This was the perfect medium for creating synthetic jewels, usually in bead form, made to look like real gemstones. Once fabrication was complete, these synthetic jewels sparkled, had luster and were lightweight. Multi-strand beaded necklaces became masterpieces in their own right at this time. With a little bit of imagination and the right kinds of beads anything was possible. Huge draped multi-strand necklaces with matching earrings and sometimes bracelets were in vogue from the late 1940s until the late 1960s. Many of the designers of the 1950s and 1960s used wonderful plastic beads in their hand manipulation of huge neckpieces. Mimi di N was one such designer who used plastic to the fullest in her designs. Turquoise and coral color plastic beads were common as well as beads coated in gold and silver to create a rich look at a lower price. Quite often, higher end pieces incorporated both plastic and glass in a particular design. Some of the designs from Miriam Haskell from this time fit into this category of plastic and glass or crystal combinations. Some designs were entirely plastic, hand-wired to create the masterpieces so coveted today.

Sarah Coventry ad displaying a variety of glass, plastic and metal jewelry from 1963.

Molded Stones

Molded plastic gemstones designed in many different colors and cuts were made by Colt's Manufacturing Company from Hartford, Connecticut. These stones were set into brooches, necklaces, bracelets, earrings and rings. They were said to be better than synthetic glass stones because they were chip resistant, had a luminous brilliance to them and they were inexpensive to manufacture. Some designers and manufacturers preferred them to glass, although plastic and glass stones were also used in combination to create wonderful pieces of costume jewelry. Sarah Coventry jewelry from the 1950s and 1960s incorporated plastic gemstones into the designs of many of the pieces offered for sale.

1950s Vicara sweater model wearing plastic bead necklaces, Glamour December, 1954.

Thermoset Designs

Mid-century modern jewelry utilizing thermo-set plastics had a distinct look. Companies like Lisner, Coro, Kramer and Trifari among others created complete parures usually consisting of a choker necklace, matching bracelet, clip earrings and sometimes a brooch made with thermo-set plastic shapes in a rainbow of colors and usually designed with a repetitive look. For example, a choker necklace and matching bracelet was composed of identical sections connected with metal links. The same design was offered in many different colors. Many of the shapes were geometric while others were leaf and flower shapes. The metal used in the setting was more creative than the plastic itself. Hundreds of examples were offered for sale season after season for at least a decade.

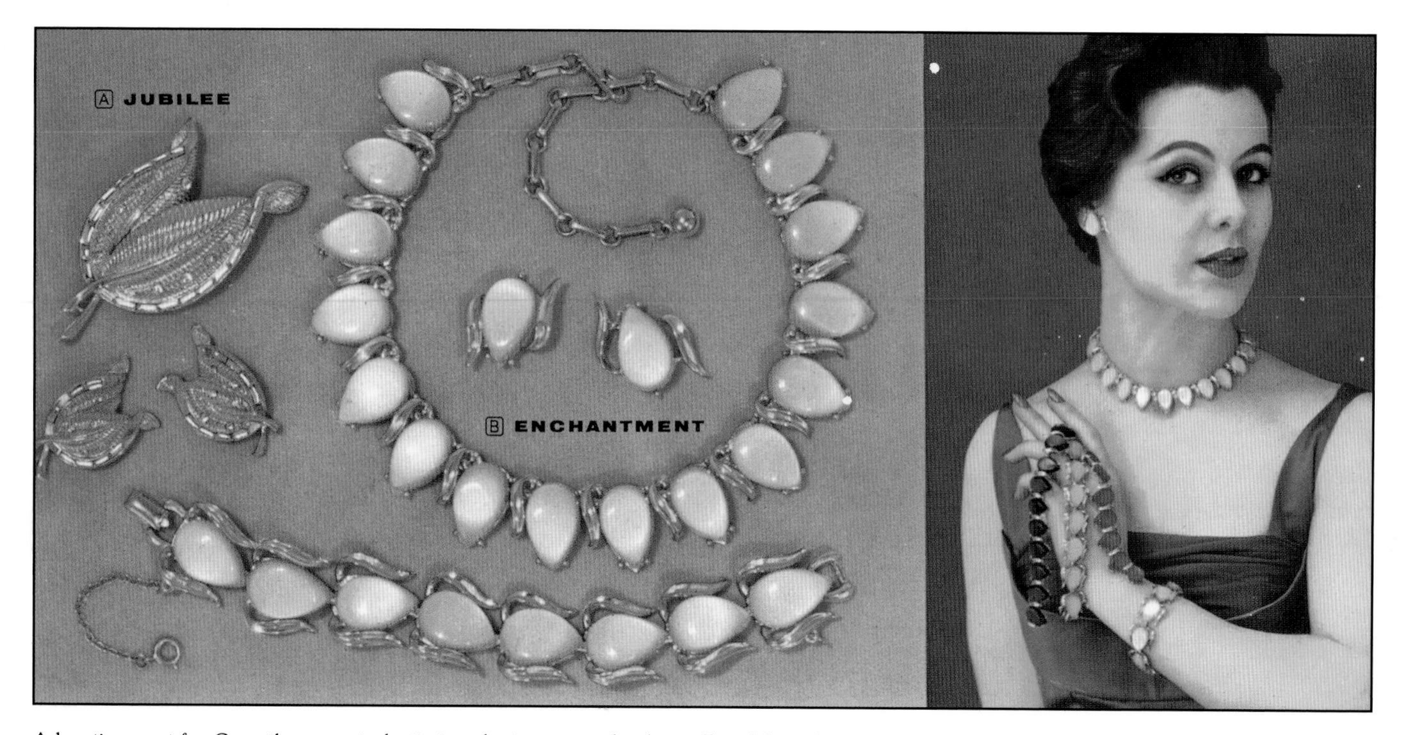

Advertisement for Coro thermoset plastic jewelry in assorted colors offered for sale in 1958.

Peach-colored thermoset plastic parure, enamel embellishment. $95 set.

Lisner orange and yellow leaf jewelry, thermoset plastic. Necklace $48; demi-parure $75

Stunning dark pink thermoset plastic bells are set into silvertone metal, unmarked. $95 set.

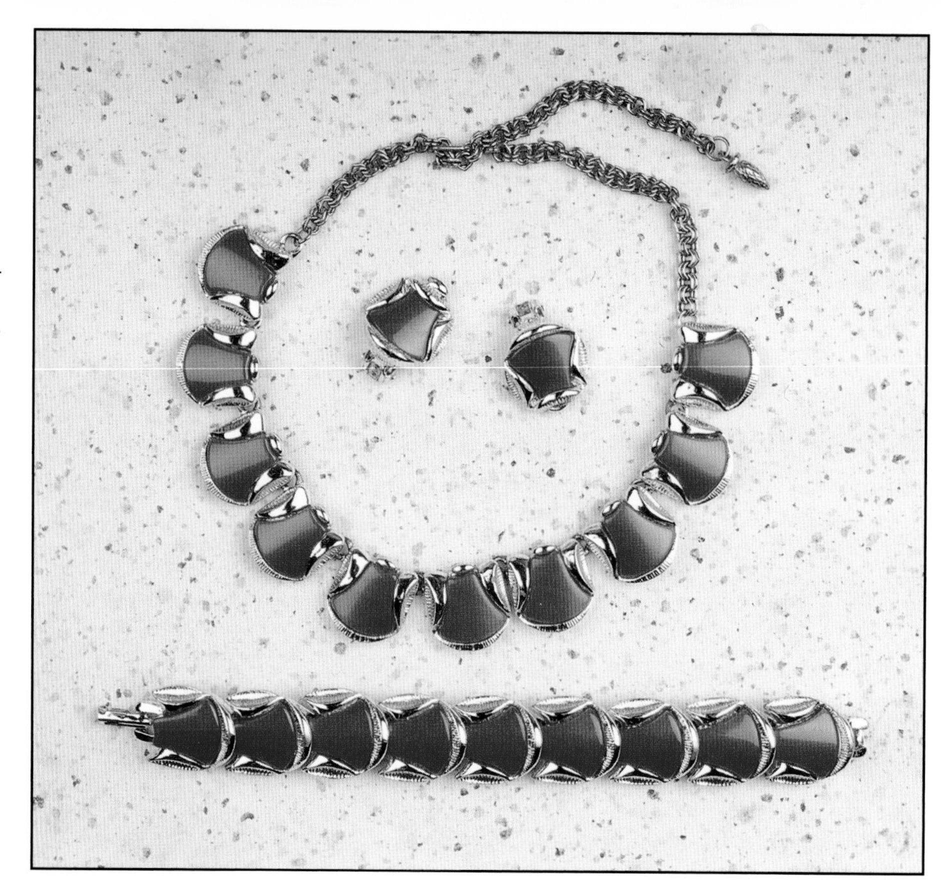

Creativity in design was evident in mid-century thermoset plastic jewelry, not only in the shape of the plastic, but the rainbow of colors that were available as well as the different metal settings. This two-toned set in goldtone metal was further enhanced with rhinestones. $95 set.

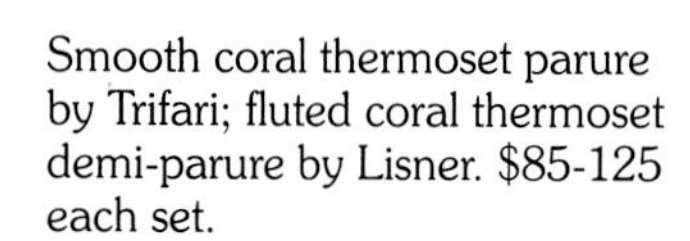

Smooth coral thermoset parure by Trifari; fluted coral thermoset demi-parure by Lisner. $85-125 each set.

Lucite

Acrylic resin, more commonly known as Lucite, had been in use since the late 1920s. In 1928 the Du Pont Company of Arlington, New Jersey introduced Lucite for dresser sets and boudoir accessories. Early Lucite was available in a wide range of color and finishes. By the 1930s, acrylic thermoplastics in crystal clear form were used for aircraft canopies and windshields. Lucite was half the weight of glass, strong, durable and best of all shatterproof. In 1937, DuPont offered methyl methacrylate molding powder, known as "Lucite" for *finer molded products*. It also became available in sheets, rods and tubes for more versatility.

Reverse-carved and hand-painted Lucite bangle bracelet. $85.

Reverse-carved Lucite hair comb, metal decoration . $95.

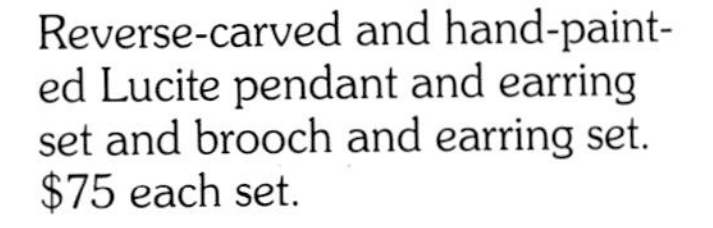

Reverse-carved and hand-painted Lucite pendant and earring set and brooch and earring set. $75 each set.

Reverse-carved and hand-painted Lucite pins and earrings in a variety of shapes and sizes. $50-85 each.

Reverse-carved and hand-painted Lucite orchid pendant and matching earring set. $75 set.

By the 1940s, clear Lucite became a popular choice for a large variety of dressing accessories for men and women as well as for jewelry. The excellent clarity of clear Lucite made the product extremely desirable. Transparent Lucite was also available in jewel tone colors. Crystal clear Lucite was often reverse carved and hand painted creating bracelets, brooches, buckles and earrings along with a host of other decorative items for the dressing table or desk.

Assorted pins, pendants and earrings made of reverse-carved Lucite. $50 each set.

Link bracelet and matching brooch, reverse-carved Lucite. $125 set.

Sometimes, in sheet form, Lucite was laminated to obtain different effects. Other times, in bead form, the Lucite was faceted to make the beads look like glass or real gemstones. Molded pieces were made in unusual shapes to suit the demand for a particular look that the designer was trying to achieve. Huge triple strand necklaces were advertised as "bogus-crystal beads" by Van S in the 1960s and available in 19 different color combinations. For example a mauve-to-purple necklace consisted of three strands, each a little different shade creating a rainbow effect in the same color group. Another common color scheme was amber tones. These necklaces retailed for $15 each and were sold in major department stores.

Reverse-carved and hand-painted Lucite brooches. $45 each.

Reverse-carved Lucite pendants. $50 each.

Lantern pin and earrings, Lucite. $45 each.

Cameo pendants and earrings, Lucite. $40 each.

Black, white and clear Lucite beads, hand-painted. $65.

Beaded necklaces, earrings, colored Lucite. $25-45 each.

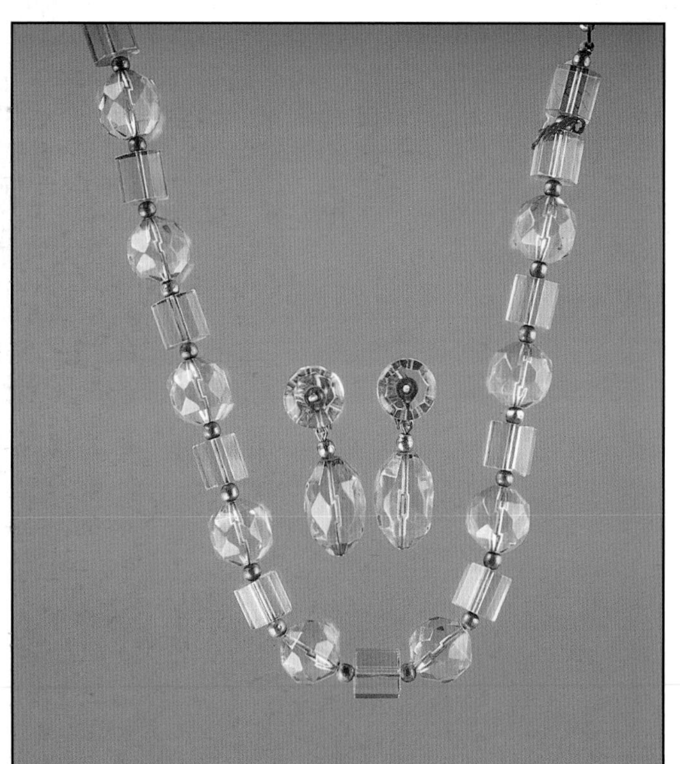

Faceted Lucite necklace and earring set. $55 set.

Opaque Lucite bead necklaces and earrings. Set $75; necklace $50.

Clear Lucite necklaces accented with goldtone chains. $45 each.

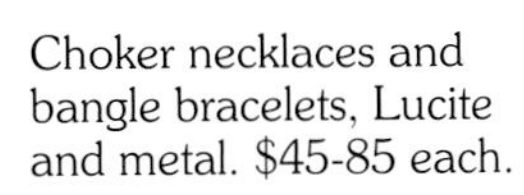

Choker necklaces and bangle bracelets, Lucite and metal. $45-85 each.

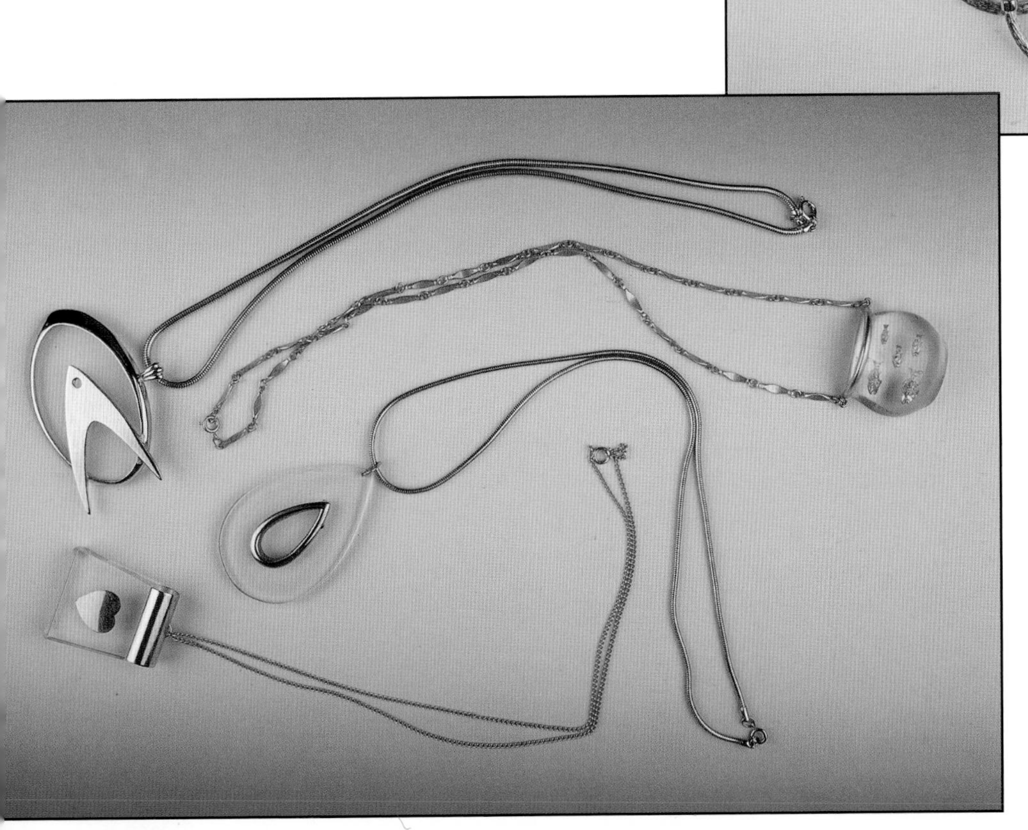

Lucite and metal pendant necklaces. $65-135 each.

Plexiglas

Modern jewelry of the 1960s incorporated Plexiglas as well as Lucite in its designs. Plexiglas was the trademark from the United States Patent Office for a thermoplastic acrylic resin manufactured by Rohm & Haas Company. Plexiglas was lightweight yet extremely strong. It could be made transparent, translucent and opaque. When it was made crystal clear, the clarity of Plexiglas was said to *rival the finest glass.* Colored Plexiglas was also very appealing and special colors were made to order. Mod jewelry of the 1960s incorporated Plexiglas in its designs. Hot pink, deep purple, acid green and fluorescent orange were some of the special colors that were created. Mod earrings were also made of strips of colored thermoplastics creating unusual shapes and made in many sizes. Lucite and Plexiglas remained popular choices for jewelry manufacture until the end of the 20th century.

CORO

Big fashion splash... River Pearls
pretend, of course
Bold... bubbly... beautiful new way
to play it cool all Summer!

Come on in . . . the fashion's fine! Coro's new River Pearls couldn't be whiter, lighter, lovelier. Two to five strands in baroque or smooth finish, from $2 to $12.50. At leading stores or write Coro Inc., N. Y. 1

Coro

Large imitation pearl necklace and matching earrings by Coro made of cellulose acetate. These pearls were offered with smooth or Baroque finishes. Vogue, June 1960.

The look of mother of pearl is very appealing in these unmarked pieces. Set $65; bracelet $38.

Two-toned parure in turquoise and lavender, unmarked. $95 set.

Marvella multi-strand plastic bead necklace resembling jet, advertised in 1960.

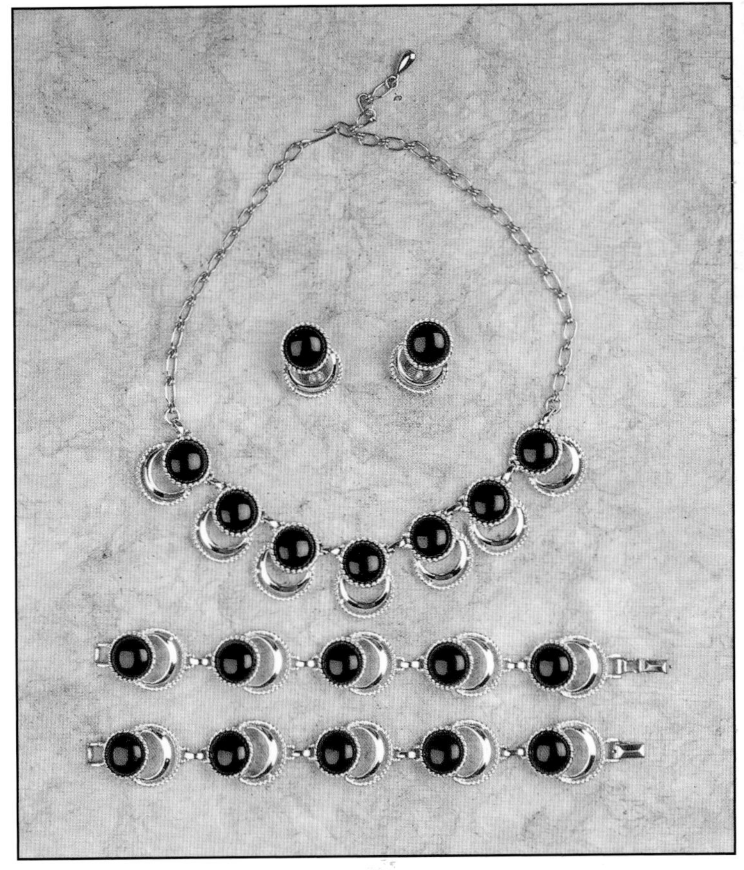

Full parure designed with concentric circles of black plastic and silvertone metal, Sarah Coventry. $135 set.

During the latter part of the 1960s, metal jewelry was beginning to dominate the fashion scene. Companies like Trifari and Monet created ropes of goldtone and silver-tone metal necklaces, sometimes enhanced with plastic beads. Huge bib necklaces were designed like lattice work and made entirely of gold-plated or silver-plated metal. Stacks of metal bangle bracelets were in vogue. Metal hoop and dangle pierced earrings became popular.

Monet white plastic jewelry collection advertised in Vogue in 1956.

Trifari white plastic jewelry collection advertised in Vogue in 1960.

Trifari bracelet collection of white plastic and gold plated metal advertised for sale in 1961.

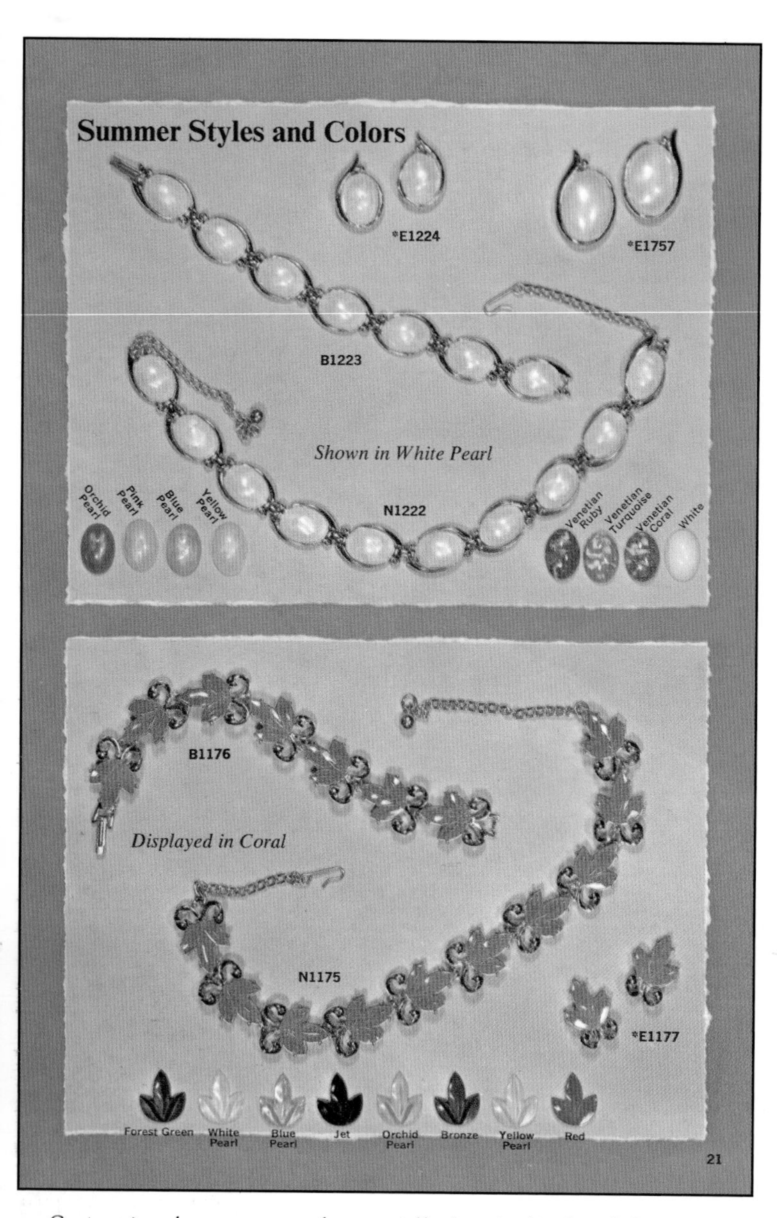

Custom jewelry you can make yourself advertised in Jewel Creations.

Although this is an ad for Mele Jewel Cases, notice the amount of plastic jewelry found in these boxes, Vogue, May 1962.

Varied shades of orange with bamboo shaped borders make this Lisner parure very appealing. $125 set.

Coro created this mid-century parure with a colorful confetti look. $145 set.

Another Coro creation in coral-colored plastic, goldtone metal and faux pearl accents. $95 set.

Necklace by Richelieu and advertised in Vogue in 1960. Notice the model wearing two plastic bangles.

Parure made of red free-form plastic beads and black plastic cabochons set into fancy silvertone links. This lovely set is unfortunately unmarked. $175 set.

Magenta moonglow circles of plastic, set into goldtone metal, created a stylish design, unmarked. $85 set.

Parure made of deep green translucent plastic leaves set in goldtone metal, unmarked. $90 set.

Demi-parure made of fluted turquoise plastic set in rhodium-plated metal, Trifari. $85 set.

Peach blossom oval plastic discs set in goldtone metal, unmarked. $80 set.

A Lisner demi-parure made to look like strawberries in shades of blue. $125 set.

A summertime delight; pink plastic shells in goldtone metal, unmarked. $75 set.

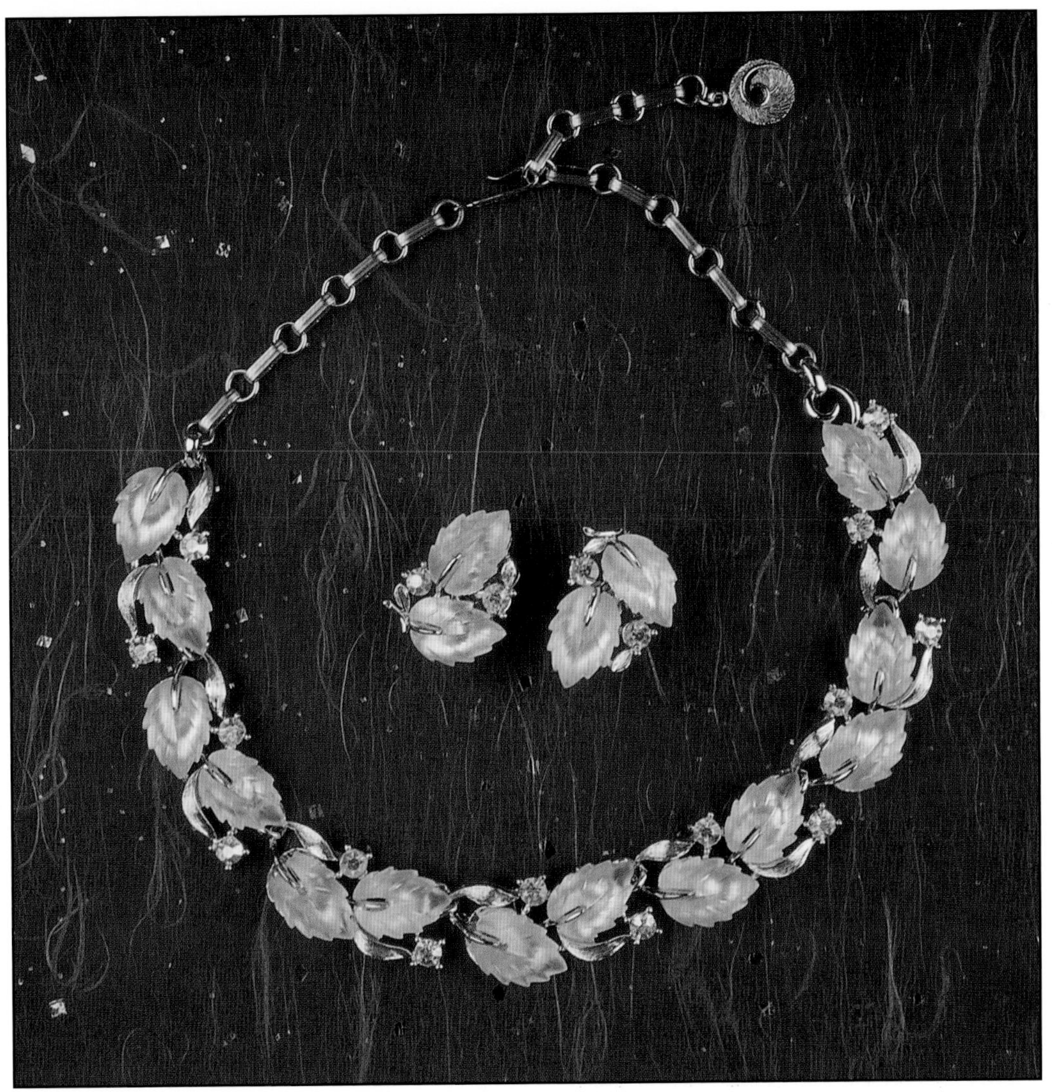

Necklace and earring set with champagne-colored plastic leaves accented with aurora borealis rhinestones, Lisner. $85 set.

Choker necklace made with black squares of iridescent confetti Lucite capped with goldtone metal. $60.

Demi-parure made of rectangular segments of confetti Lucite in goldtone metal, Coro. $75 set.

Confetti Lucite in turquoise and coral accented with metal scrolls and rhinestones. $35-60 each.

Aqua confetti Lucite squares in silvertone metal. $65 set.

Choker necklace, matching bracelet made of ovals of confetti Lucite, unmarked. $95 set.

Large and ornate confetti Lucite bracelet accented with rhinestones. $145.

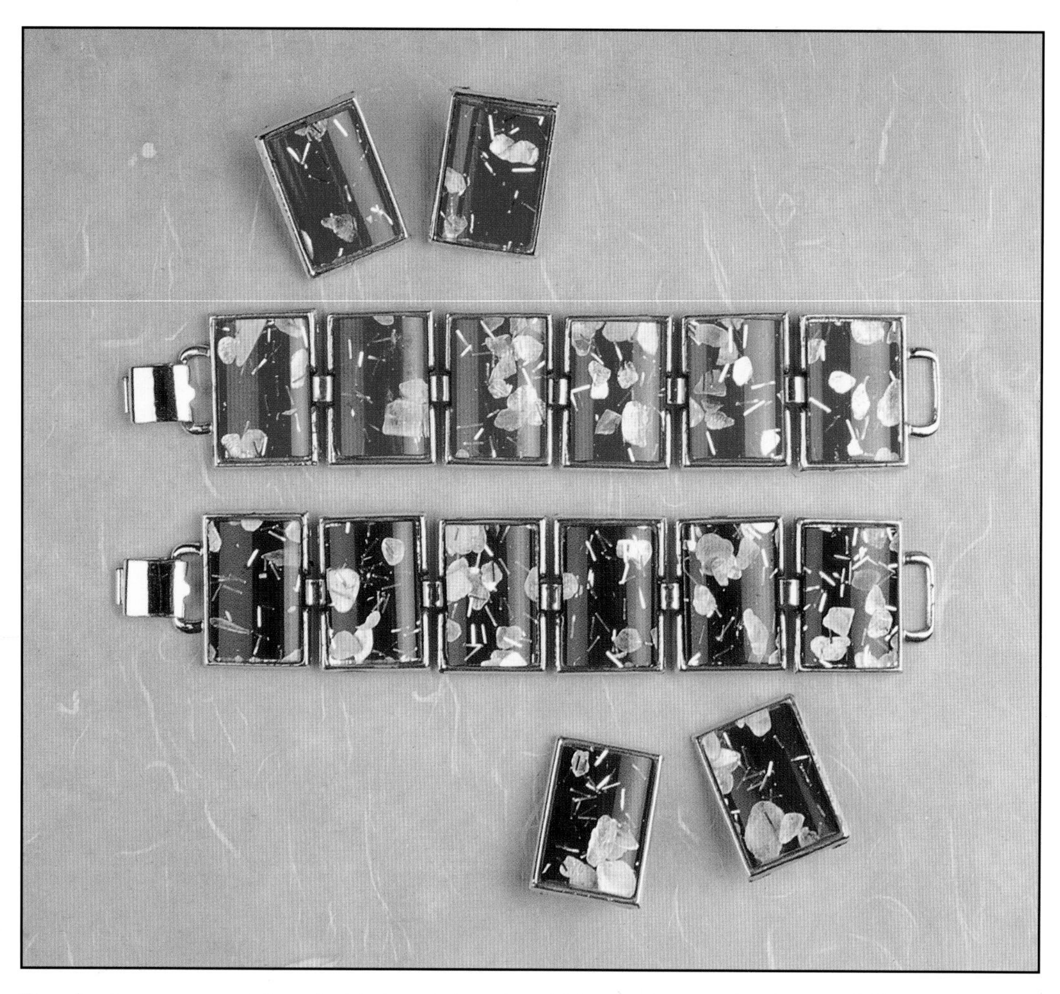

Two demi-parures consisting of wide bracelets and matching earrings made of red and blue confetti Lucite. $95 each set.

Assortment of mid-century plastic jewelry designed in a variety of shapes and pretty pastel colors. $30-65 each.

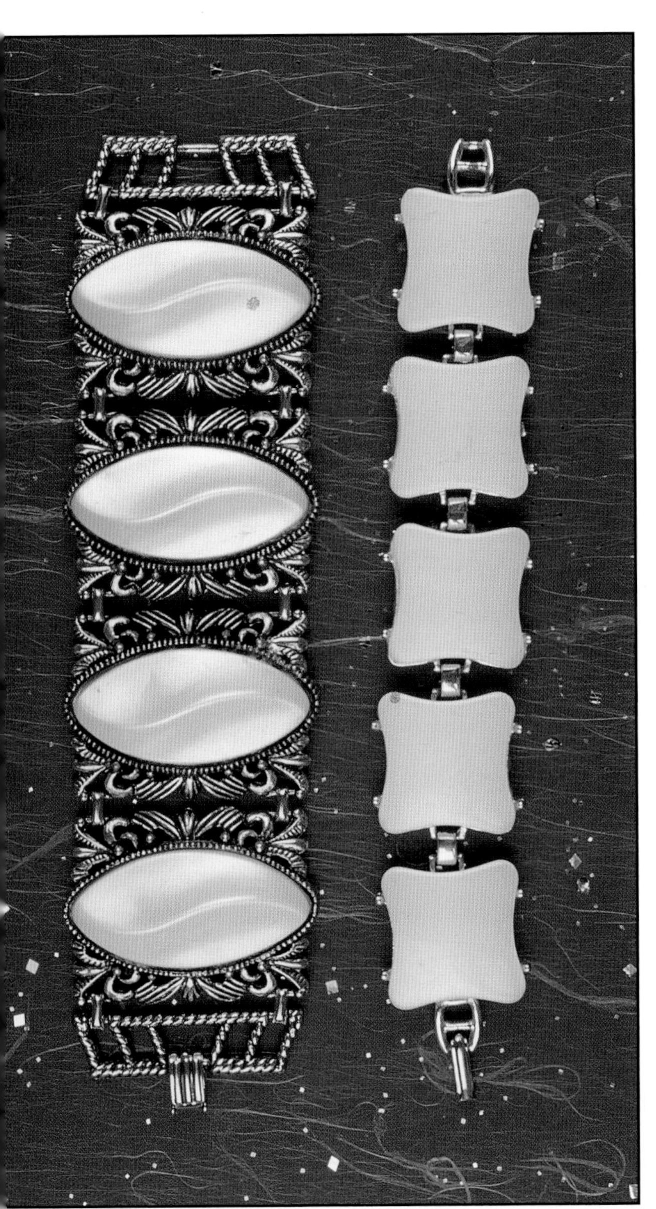

Pearl-like plastic bracelets designed from simple to elaborate. $65-135 each.

Bracelet and earring demi-parure in two-toned plastic. $75 set.

Bracelets designed with blue plastic leaves in silvertone metal and purple plastic leaves in goldtone metal. $55 each.

Two demi-parures designed with turquoise plastic and silvertone metal, Coro. $85 each set.

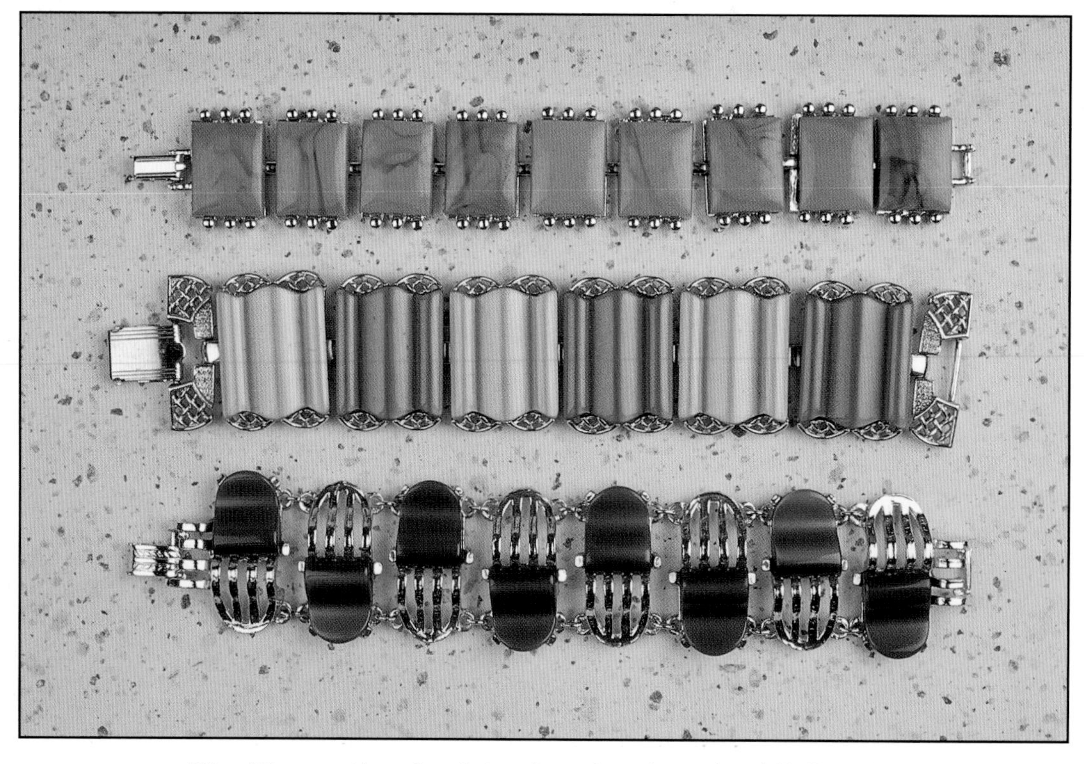

Trio of thermoset bracelets designed simple and complex. $40-65 each.

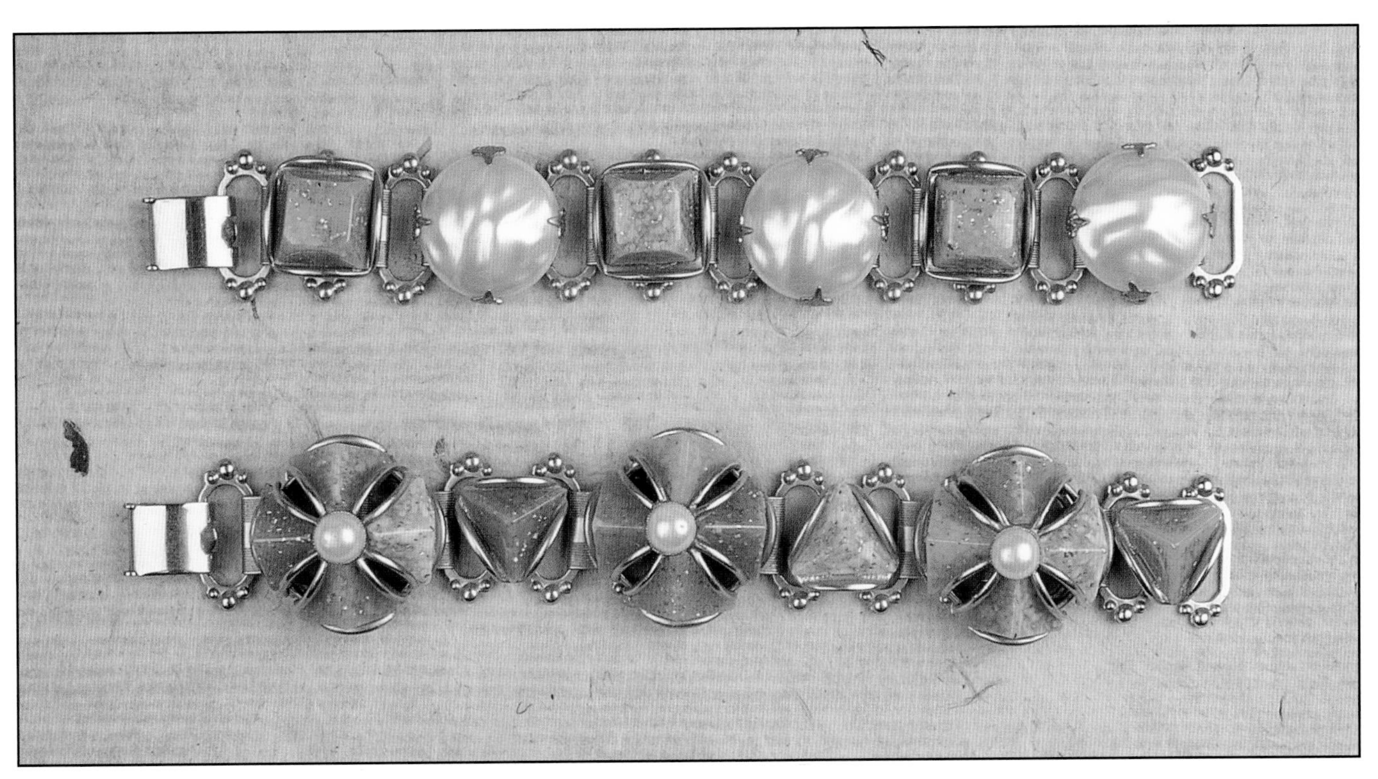

Two multi-colored confetti Lucite bracelets accented with faux pearls. $40-55 each.

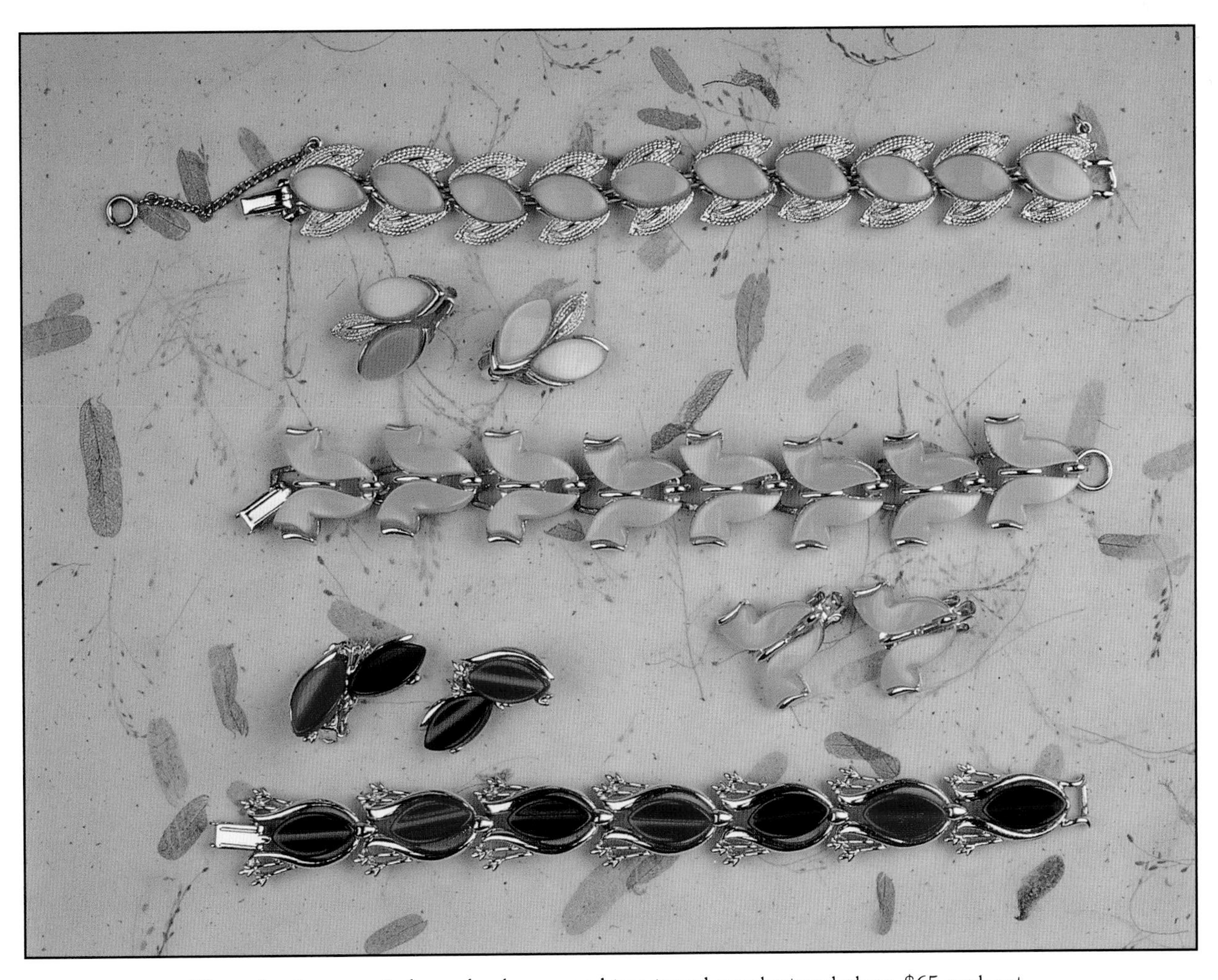

Three demi-parures in lavender, lemon and two-toned eggplant and plum. $65 each set.

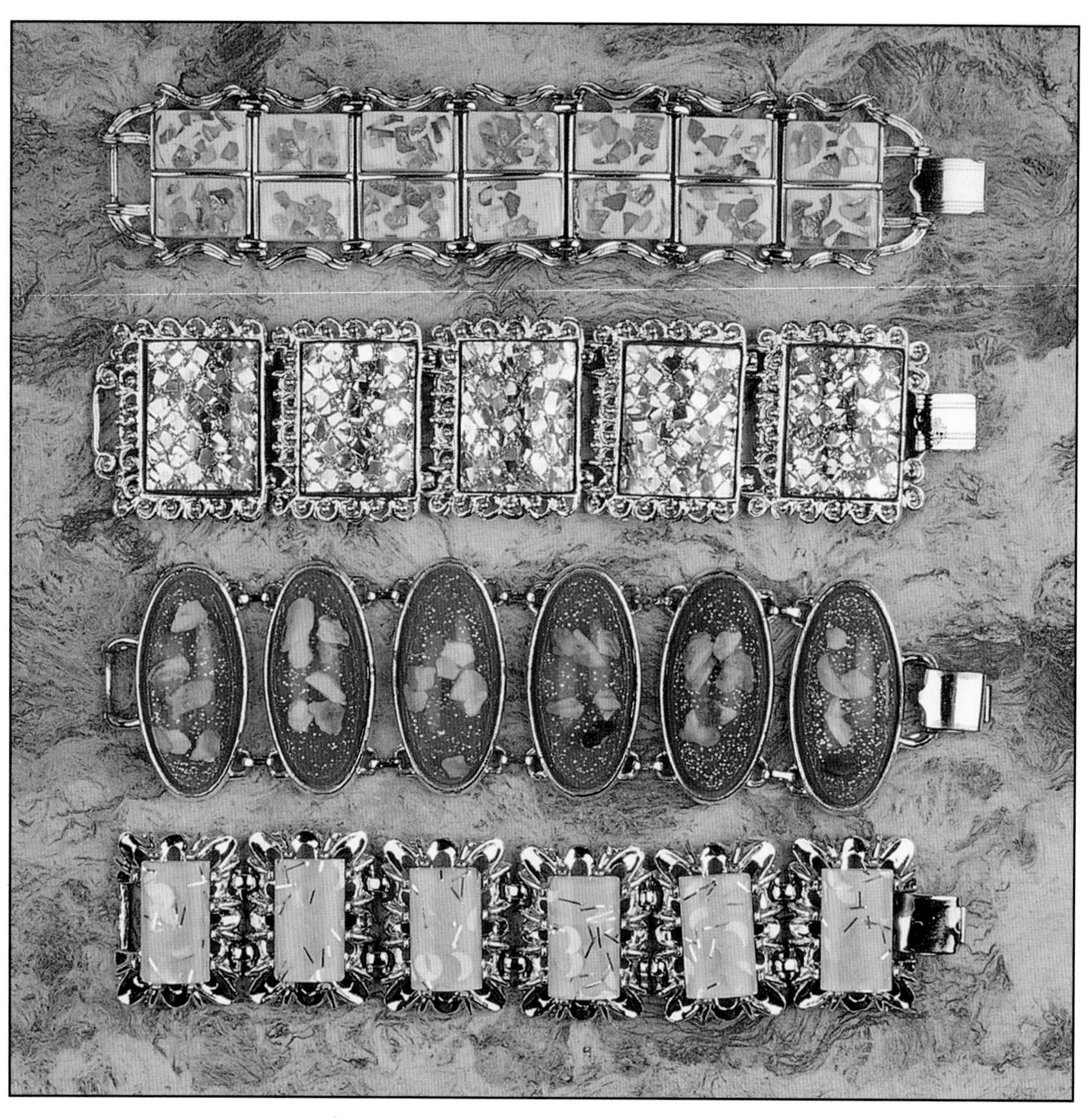

These bracelets were designed with a larger scale than most but ever so appealing. Notice how varied the Lucite is in composition as well as shape and color. $85-100 each.

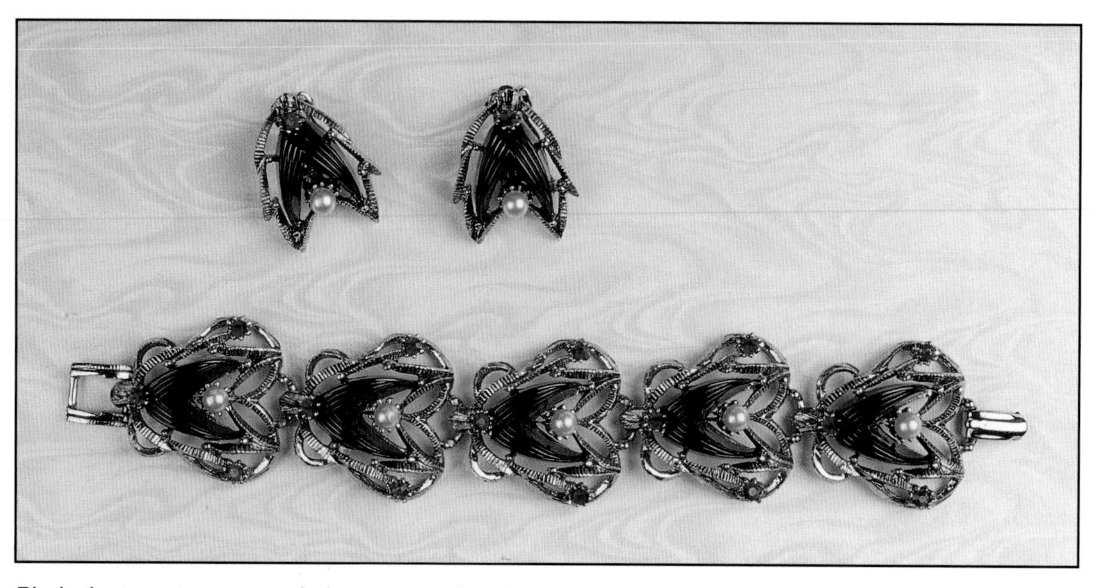

Black plastic set into antiqued silvertone metal, with pearl and stone accents, created a striking design for this demi-parure. $75 set.

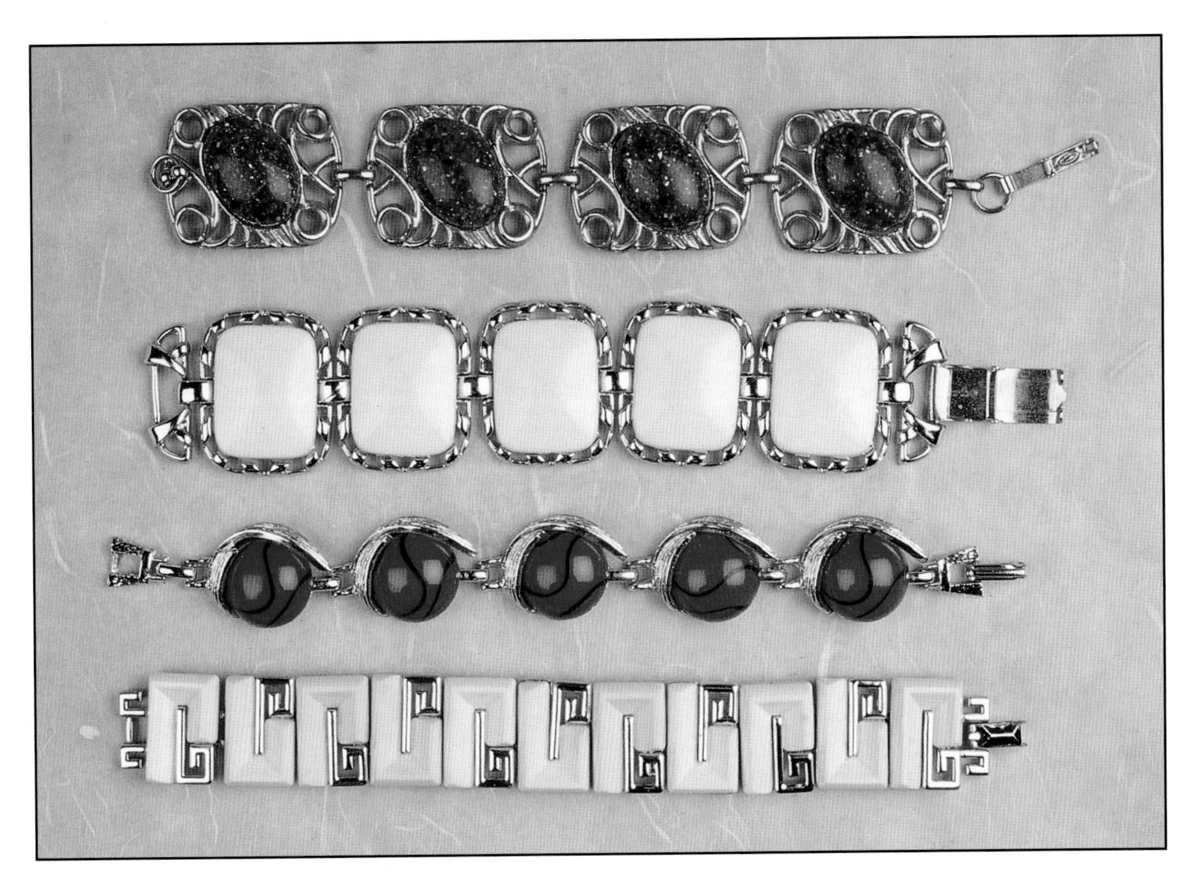

Four bracelets,
Coro and Lisner.
$38-48 each.

Cone-shaped plastic in melon and white was a unique mid-century design for this demi-parure. $80 set.

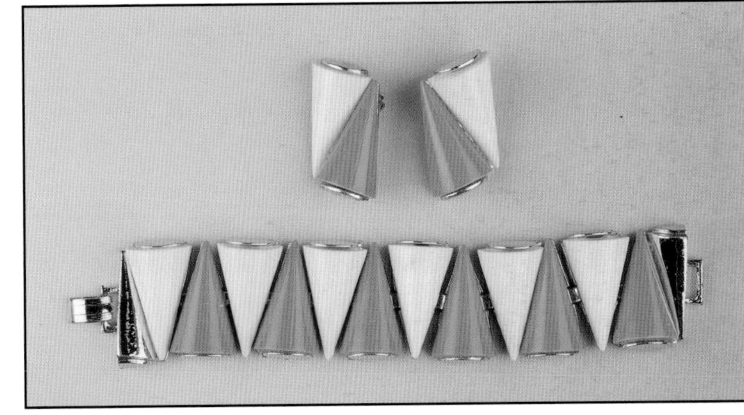

Grand parure consisting of pendant necklace, bracelet, earrings and ring designed with fancy metalwork over thermoset plastic. $150 set.

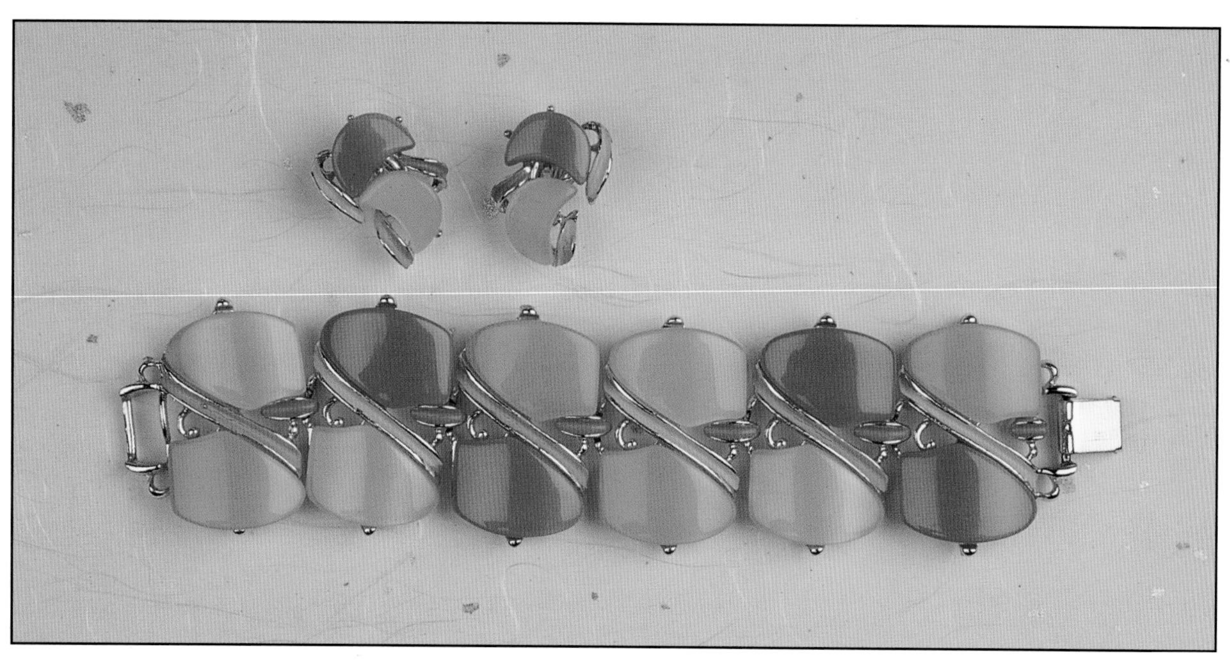

Tangerine, lime and orange with a touch of enamel was a wonderful design for this summertime demi-parure. $85 set.

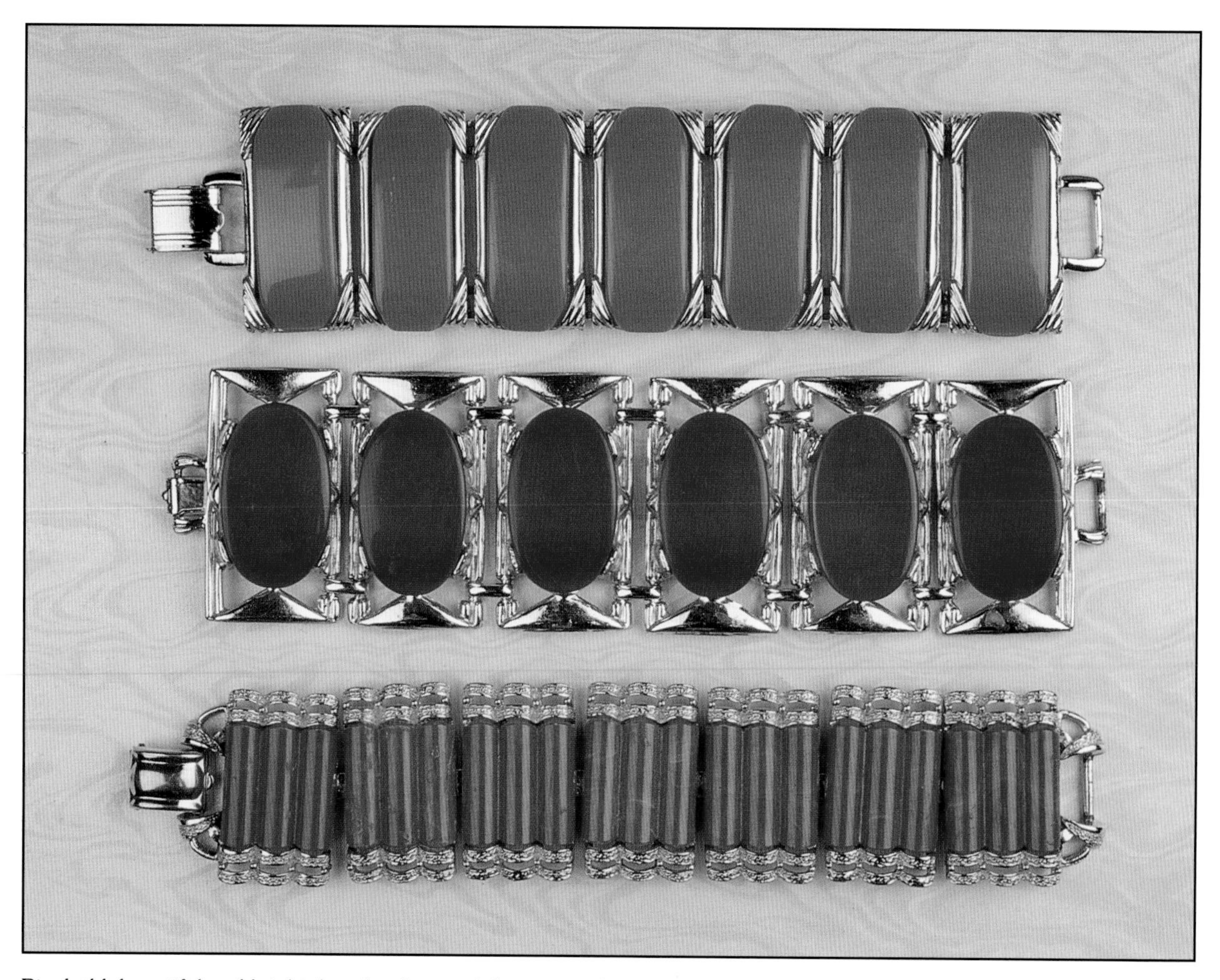

Big, bold, beautiful and bright describe these red thermoset plastic bracelets. The bracelet at the bottom is marked Coro. $65-85 each.

Pretty in pink best describe these smooth and faceted plastic bracelets and a pin duo. $30-48 each.

Basic rectangles in powder blue and canary yellow were used to design eye catching mid-century modern bracelets and matching earrings. $20-50 each.

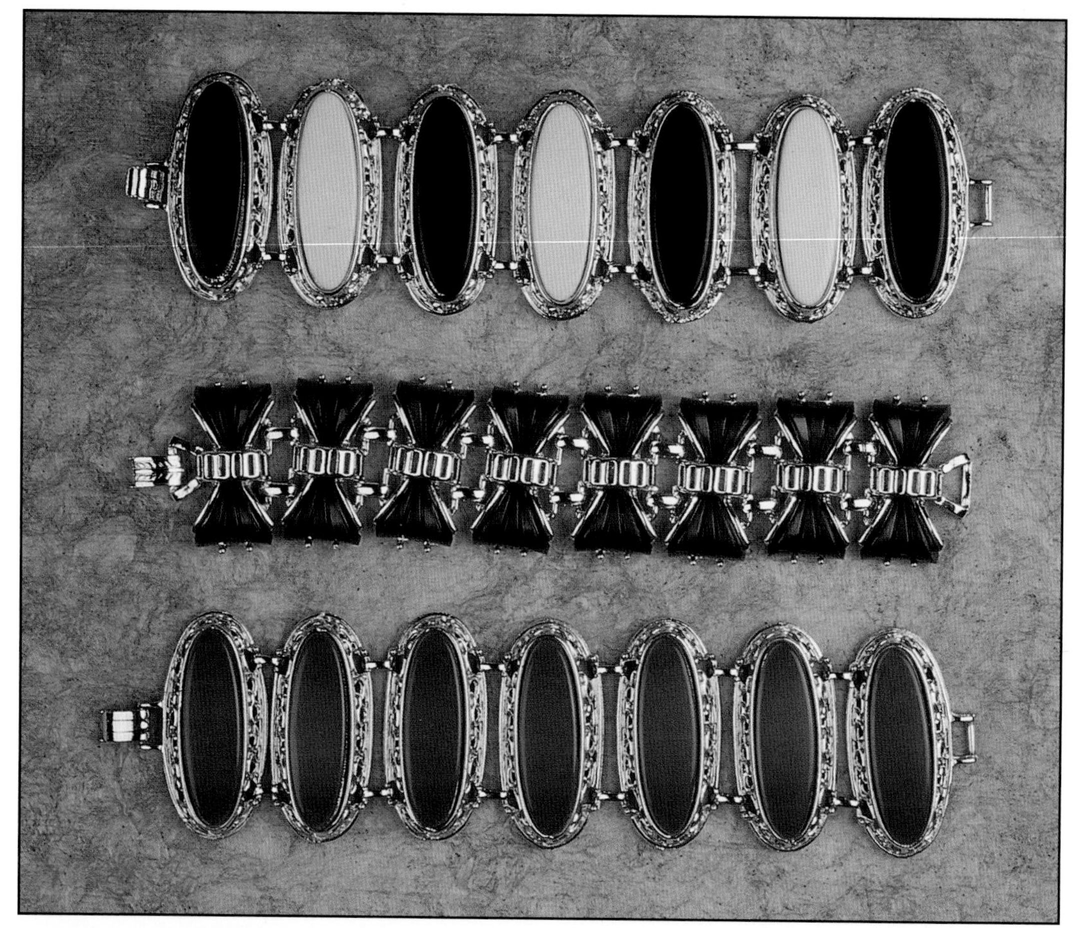

Bow shapes in plastic coupled with elongated ovals provide interesting form in mid-20th century design. $65-85 each.

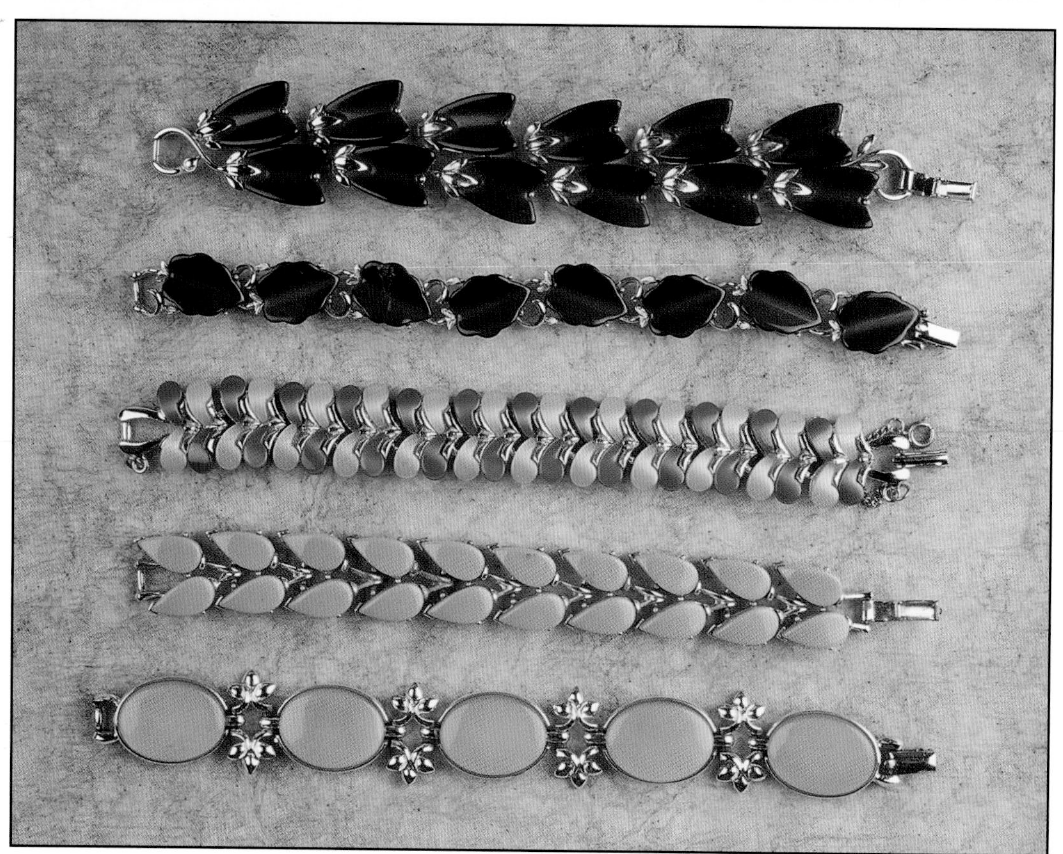

Eye candy worn on the wrist in shades of blue, green and turquoise. $40-55 each.

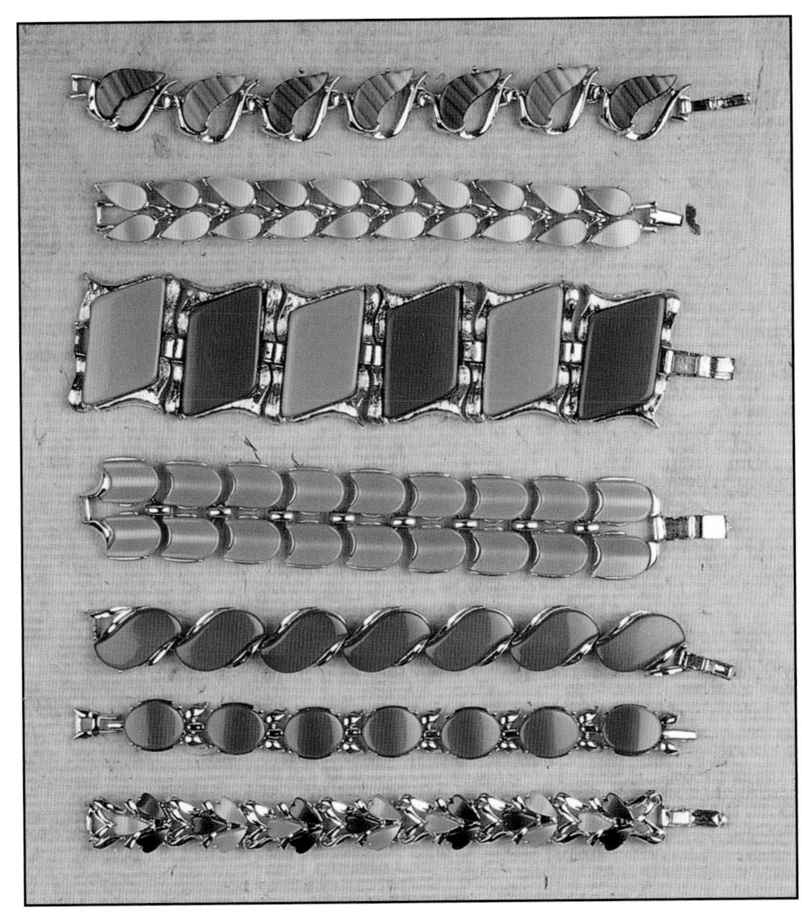

More eye candy for the wrist in earth tones. $35-75 each.

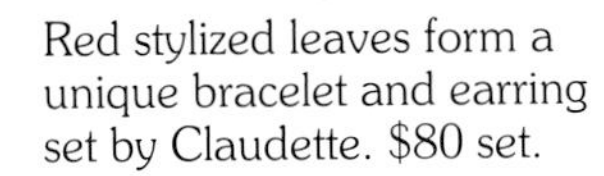

Red stylized leaves form a unique bracelet and earring set by Claudette. $80 set.

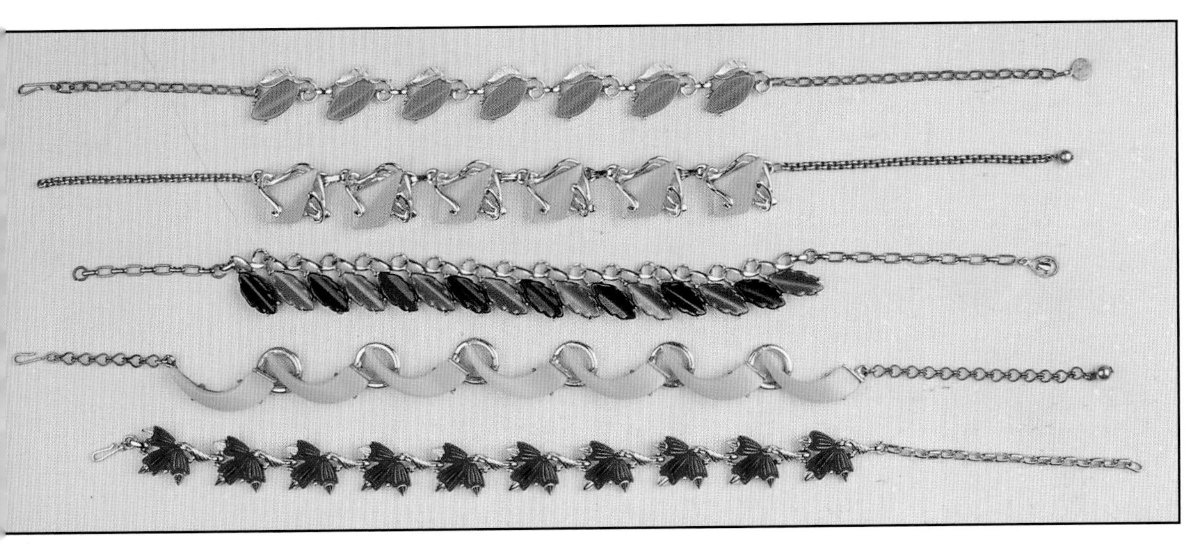

Choker necklaces made with pastel and bold-colored thermoplastics. The red fluted necklace is marked Marvella. $38-68 each.

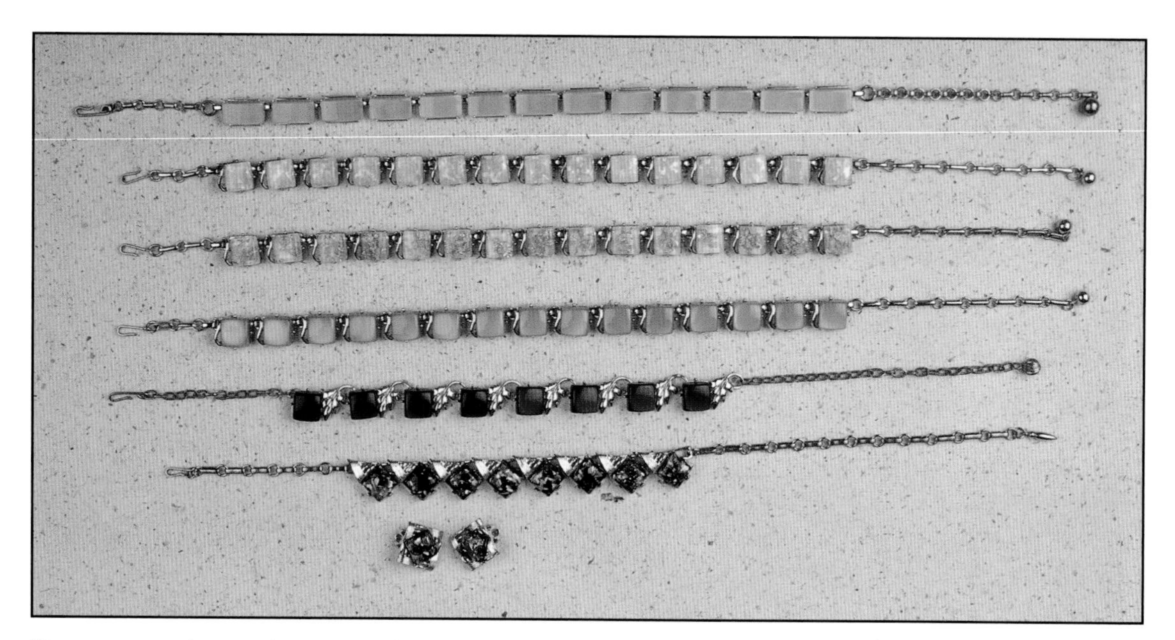

Fun squares and rectangles were used to design necklaces and earrings made of solid color as well as confetti Lucite. $20-50 each.

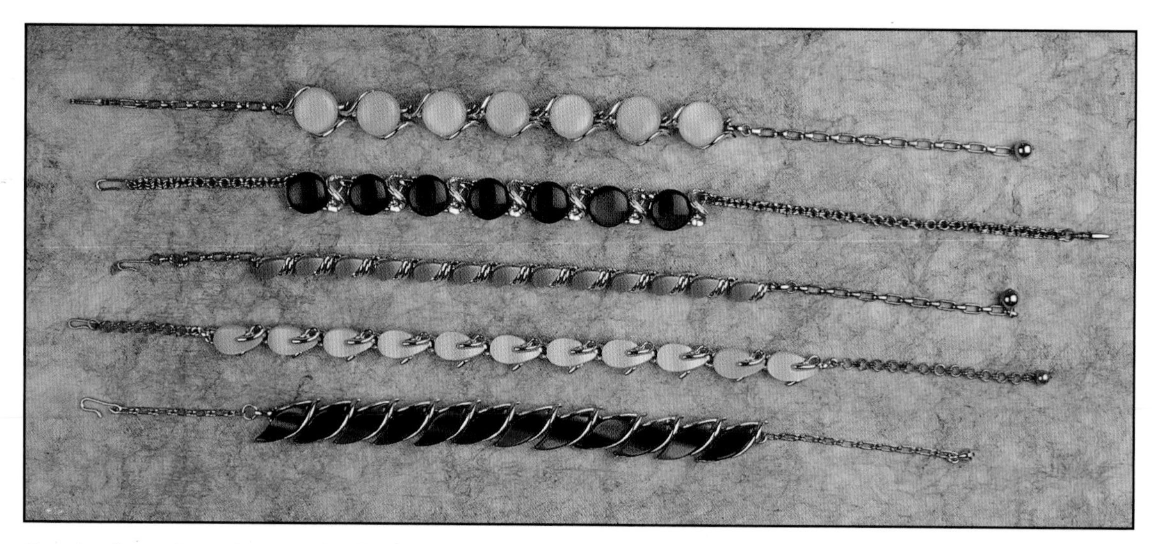

Ranging from plain white circular discs to leaf-shaped jewel tones, these plastic choker necklaces really make a statement. $30-60 each.

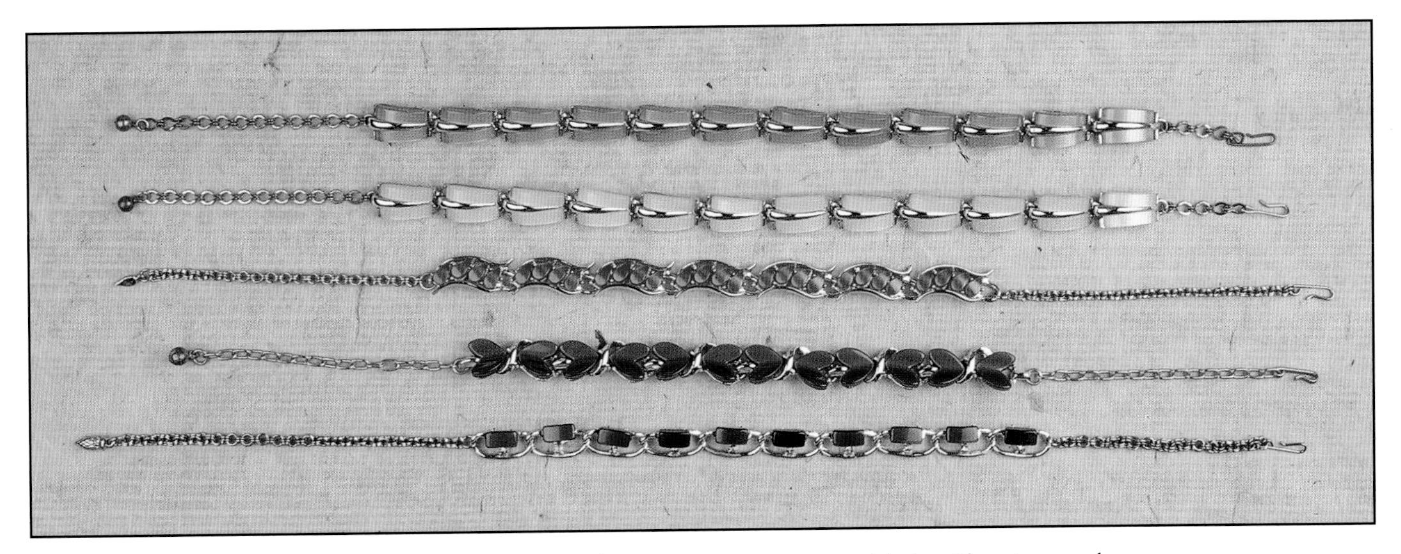

Rectangles, teardrops and heart-shapes create even more variety in mid century modern plastic jewelry. $30-48 each.

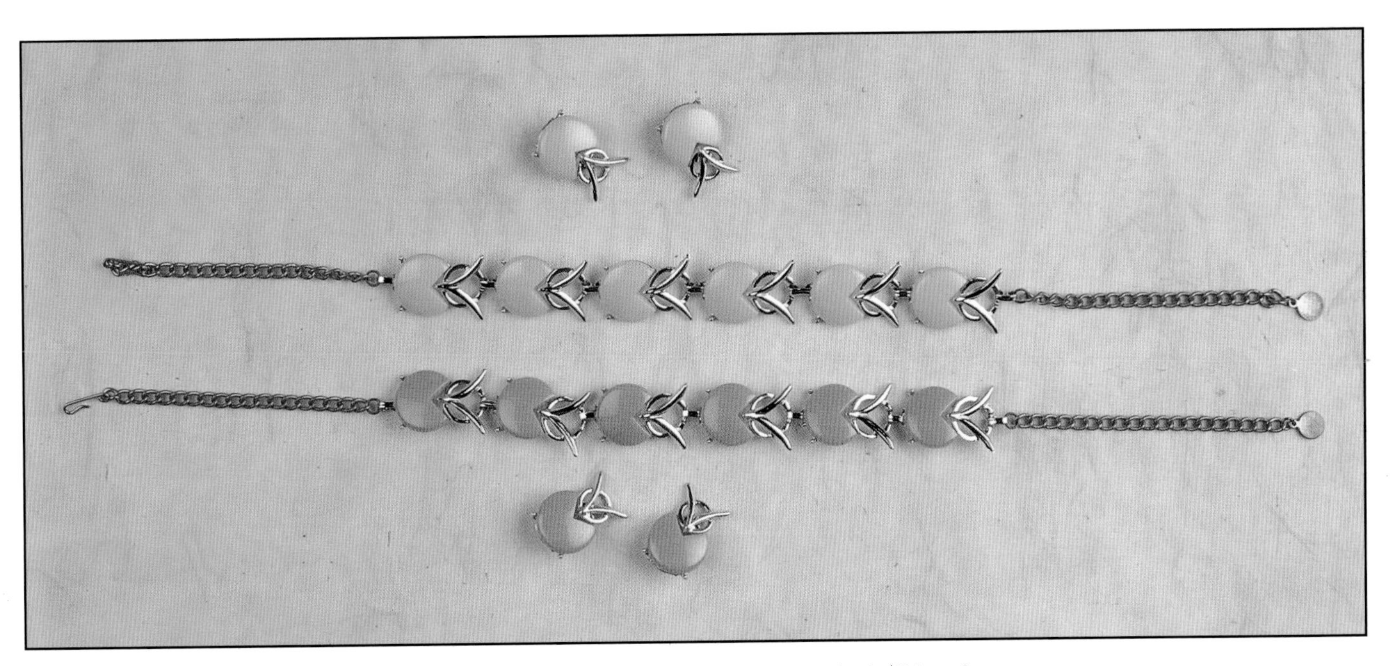

Two demi-parures in lemon and melon, unmarked. $50 each set.

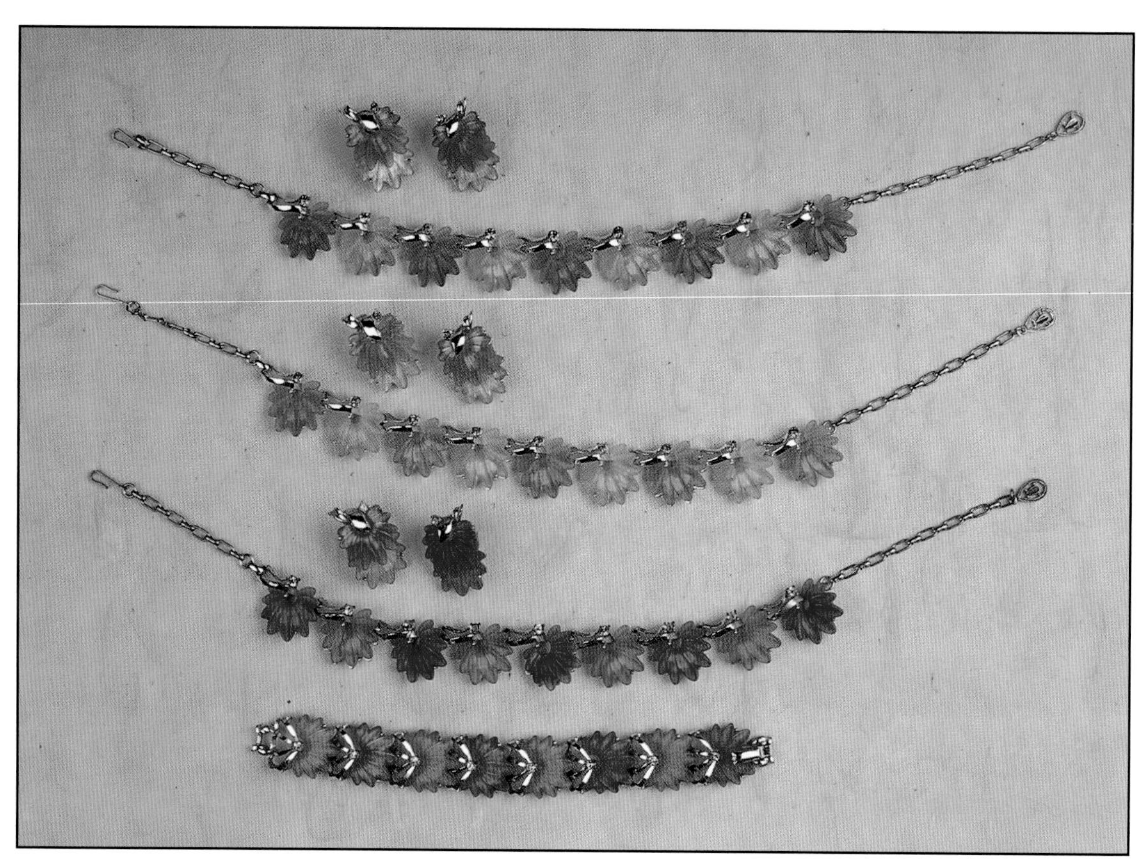

Leafy parures in light and dark translucent plastic are accented with rhinestones.
$20-60 each.

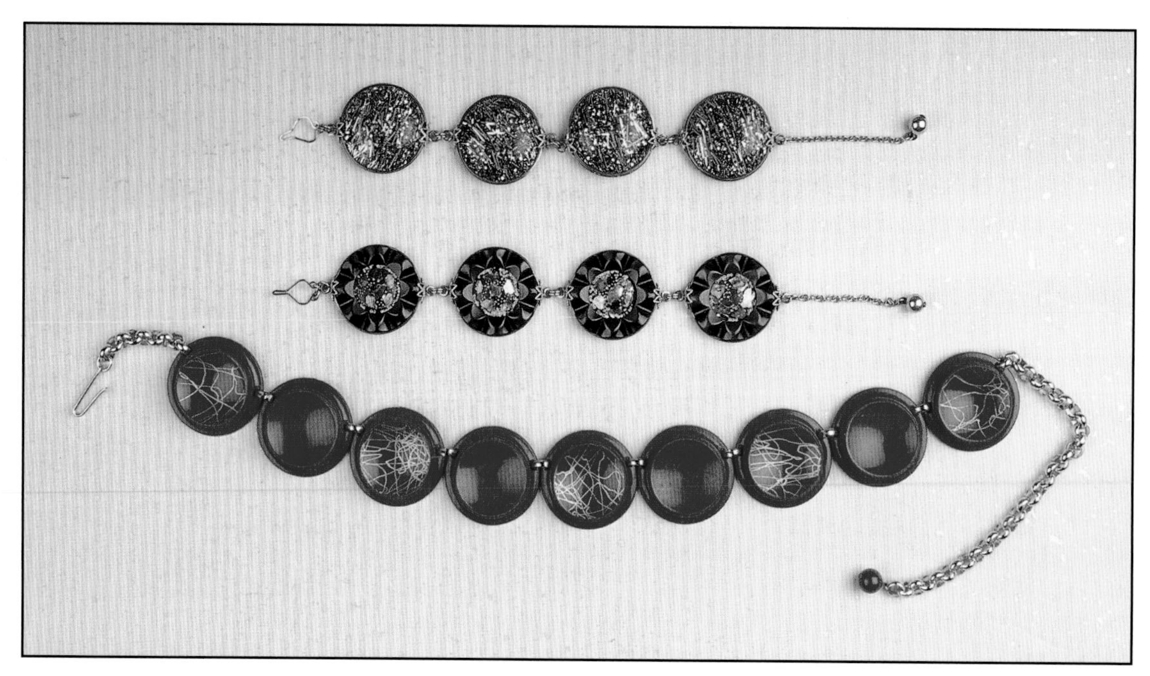

Confetti Lucite bracelets set in gold-filled metal; red plastic necklace marked Western Germany.
$35-50 each.

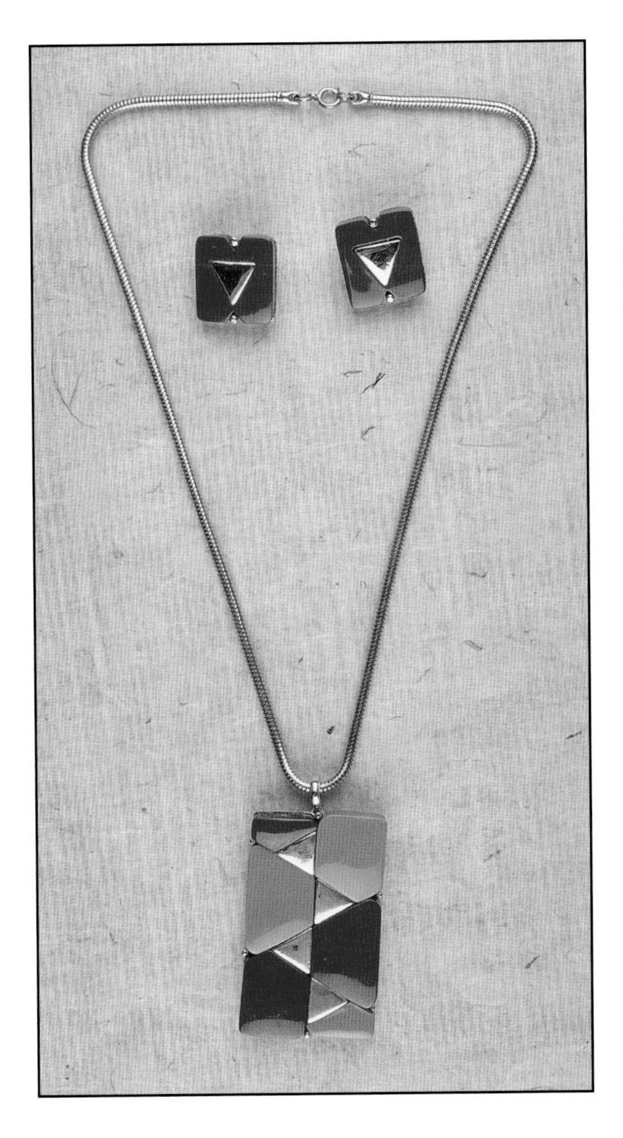

Rust and salmon geometric pendant suspended from serpentine chain accompanied by matching earrings, unmarked. $75-100 set.

Oblong brooch set with rippled red plastic; leafy pin and earring set marked Star. $30-60 each.

Expansion and clamper bracelets in great summertime colors and color combinations. $48-65 each.

Two confetti Lucite clamper bracelets; one with added sea-shells. $65-85 each.

Gold confetti Lucite and shell clamper bracelet. $85.

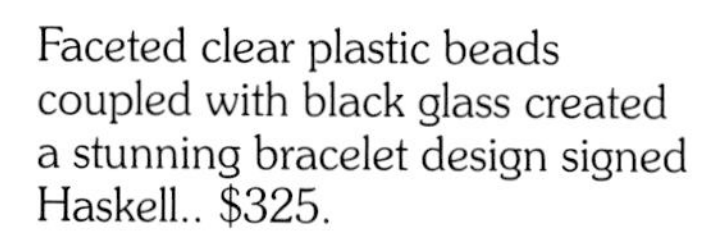

Faceted clear plastic beads coupled with black glass created a stunning bracelet design signed Haskell.. $325.

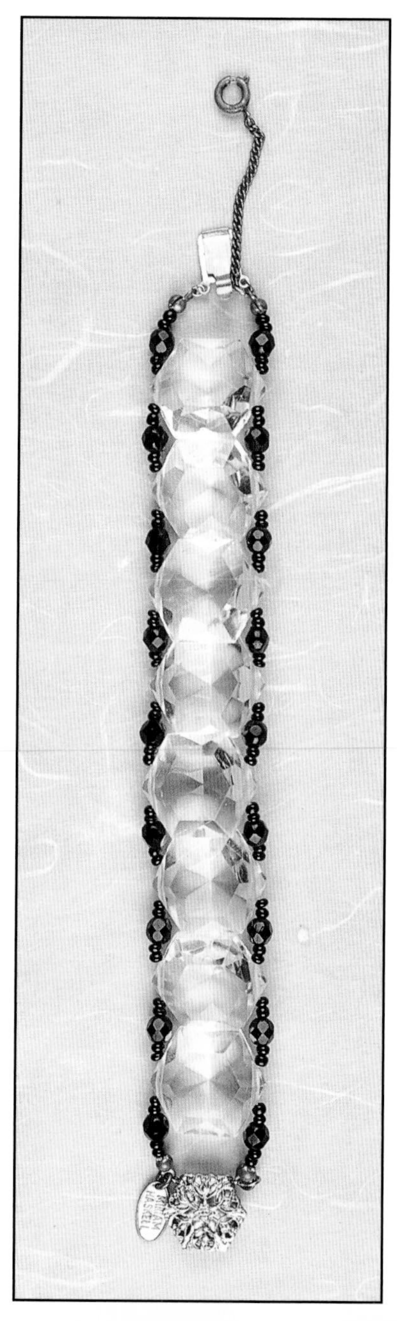

Unusual and colorful plastic clip earrings with metal accents. $15-25 each pair.

Pastel pink clip earrings with goldtone embellishments. $20-35 each pair.

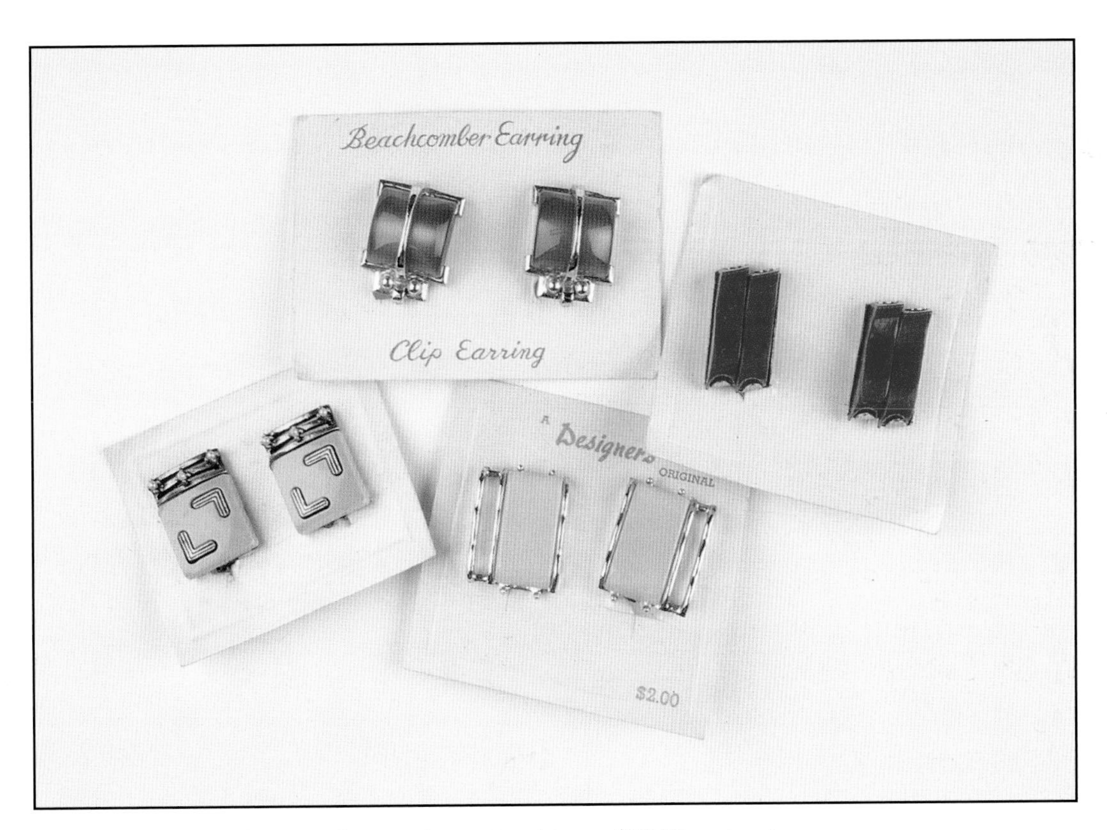

Clip earrings made of thermoplastic in deeper jewel tones. $20-30 each pair.

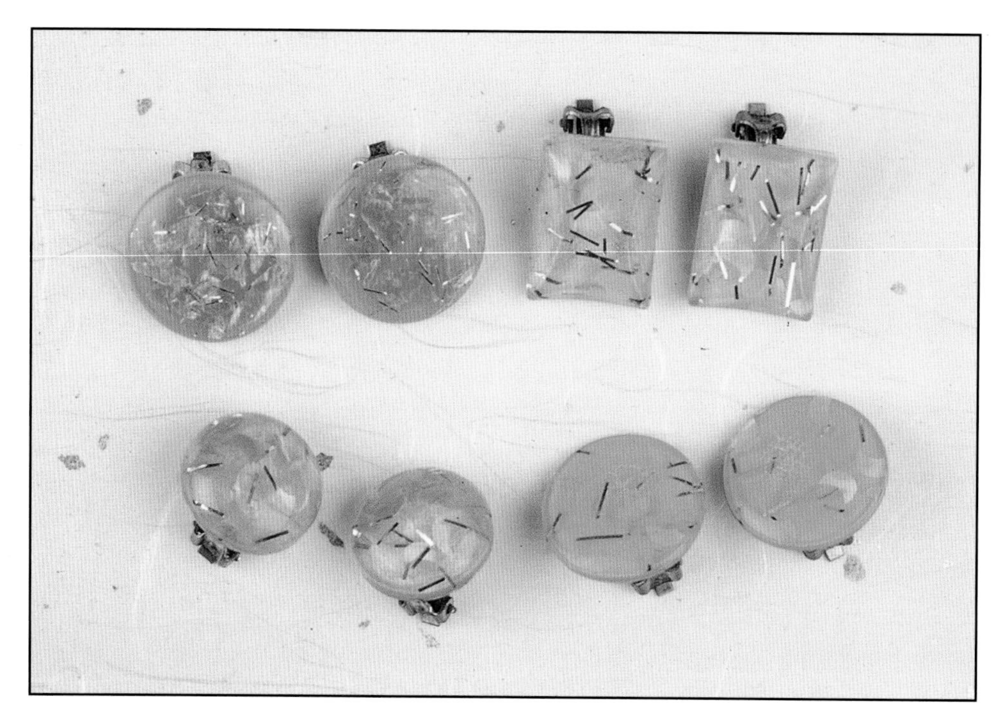

Confetti Lucite clip earrings in pastel colors. $25-35 each pair.

Variations in confetti Lucite from silver, gold and multi-color threads to tiny gold stars. $25-40 each pair.

Lovely mix of glass and assorted plastics were used to created this bracelet and earring set with lots of appeal. $75-90 set.

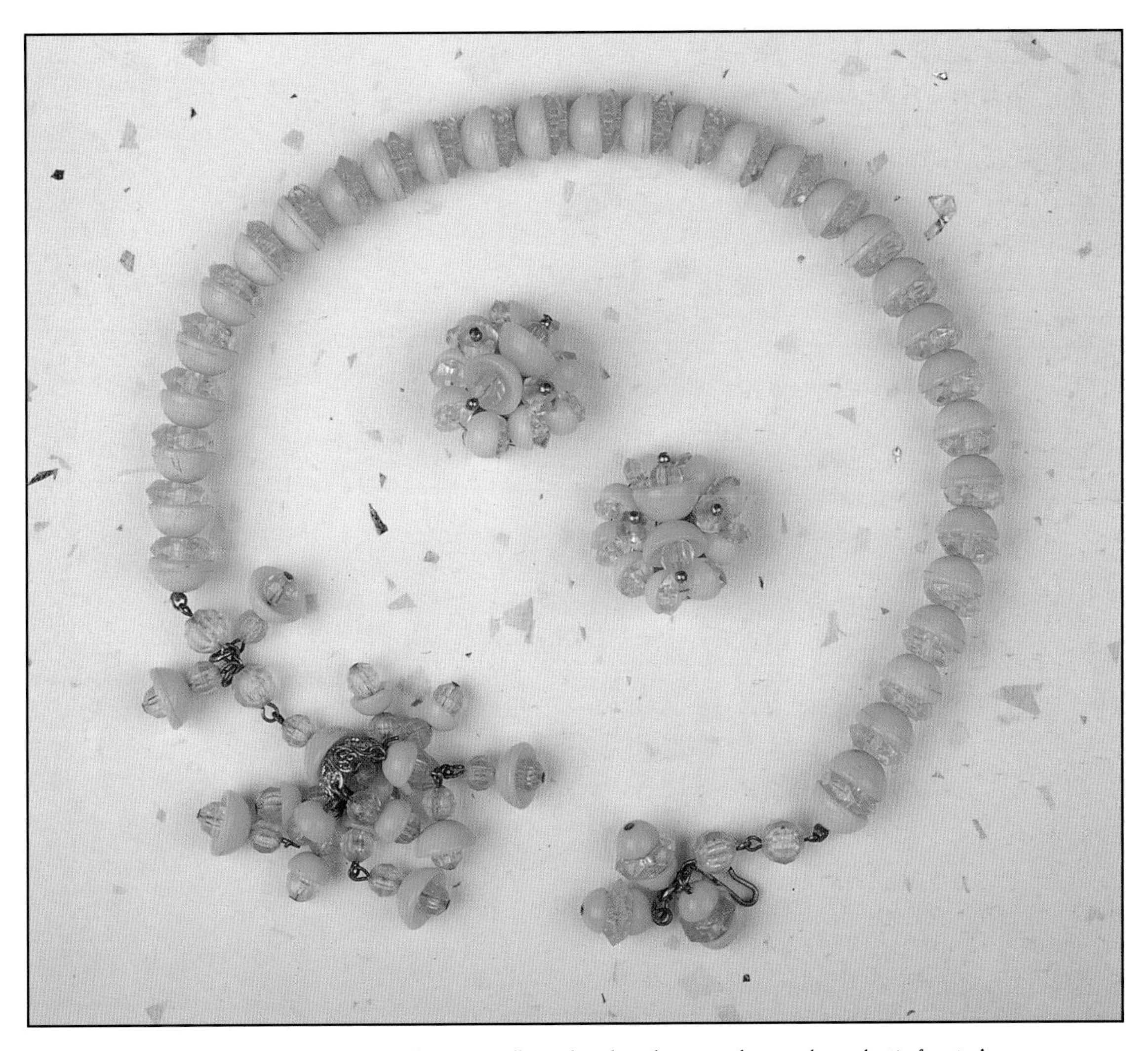

Lariat-style necklace and clip earrings of sunny yellow glass beads capped over clear plastic faceted beads. This set is similar to early unsigned Haskell jewelry. $150-185 set.

Thermoset plastic daisy necklace and earring set. $75-100 set.

Thermoset plastic hinged bangles and matching clip earrings in black with black stones and cream with aurora borealis rhinestones. $250 each set.

Thermoset plastic clip earrings set with rhinestones in different colors, shapes and sizes still on their original presentation cards. $40-75 each.

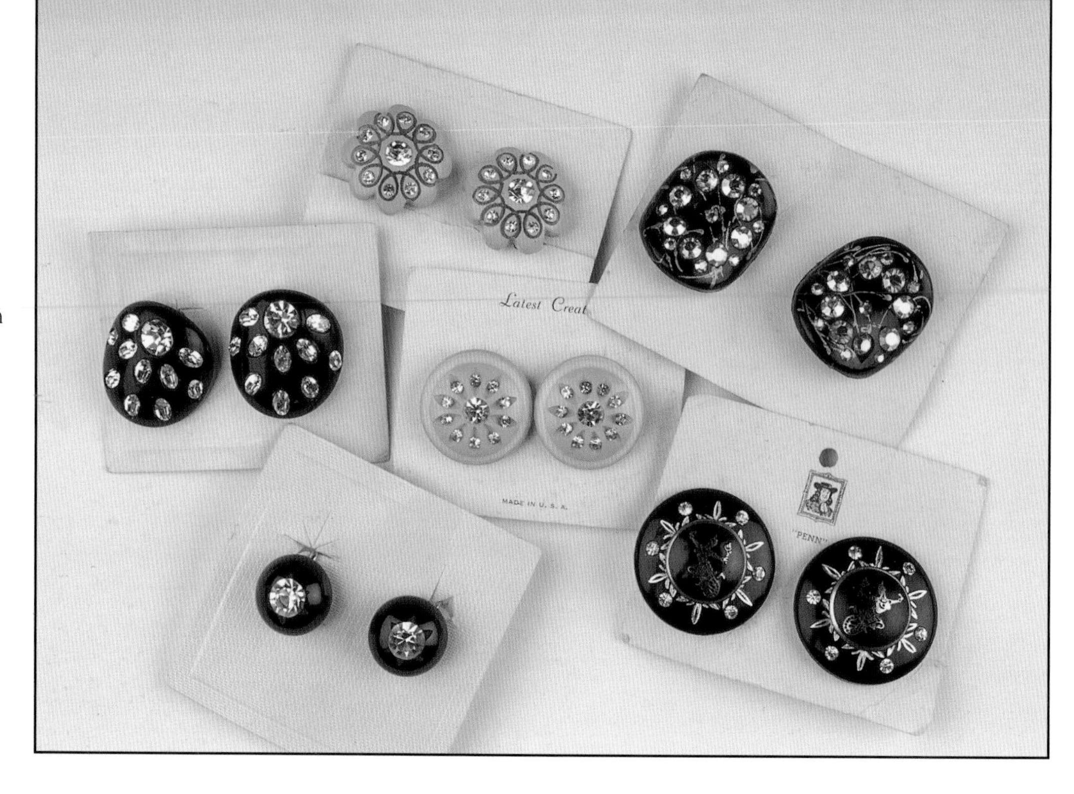

Plastic sunglasses embellished with rhinestones. $100-150 each.

Unusually faceted triple strand turquoise plastic bead necklace with matching earrings, Western Germany. $40-50 set.

Sunny yellow double strand plastic bead necklace and earring set, Germany. $40-50 set.

Fifteen strands of elongated pink plastic beads and pearl spacers were used to create this lovely necklace and earring set marked Hong Kong. $38-48 set.

From candy apple red to iridescent, these plastic beads resemble glass. $40-60 set.

Chunky triple strand necklace and earring set made of blue and green faceted and graduated Lucite beads. $50-75 set.

Four strand faceted and graduated Lucite beads in lavender. $45-65.

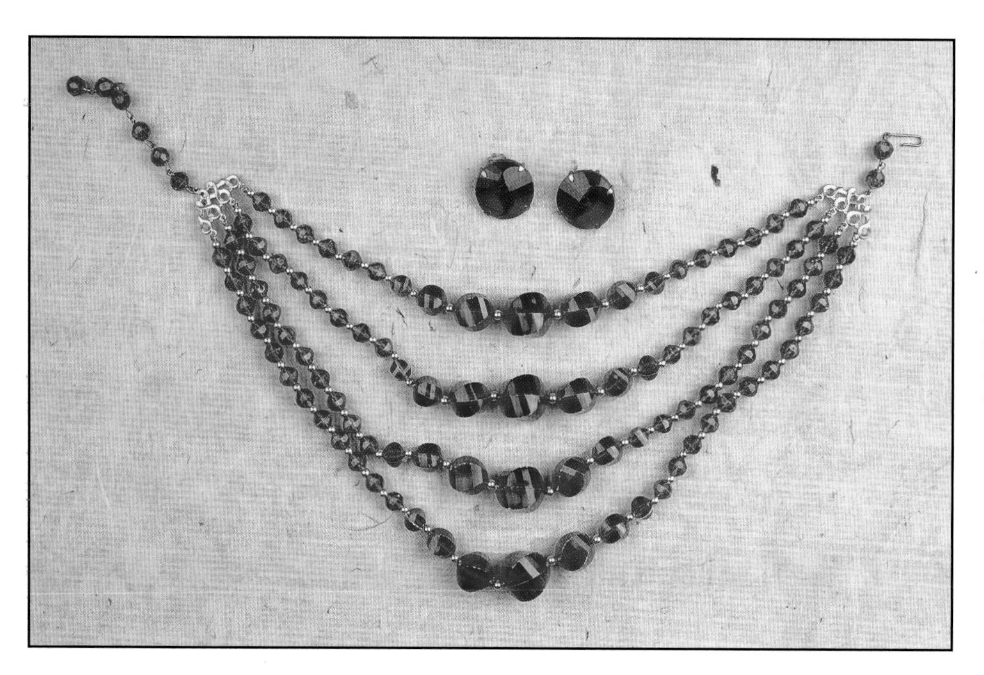

Four strand faceted and graduated Lucite bead necklace and earring set in candy apple red. $55-75 set.

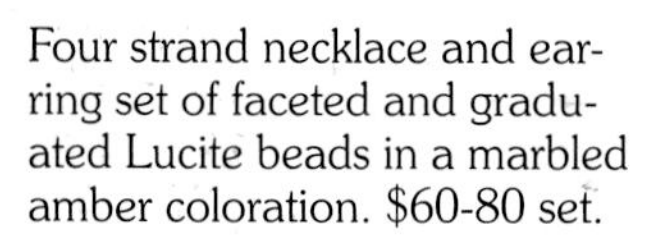

Four strand necklace and earring set of faceted and graduated Lucite beads in a marbled amber coloration. $60-80 set.

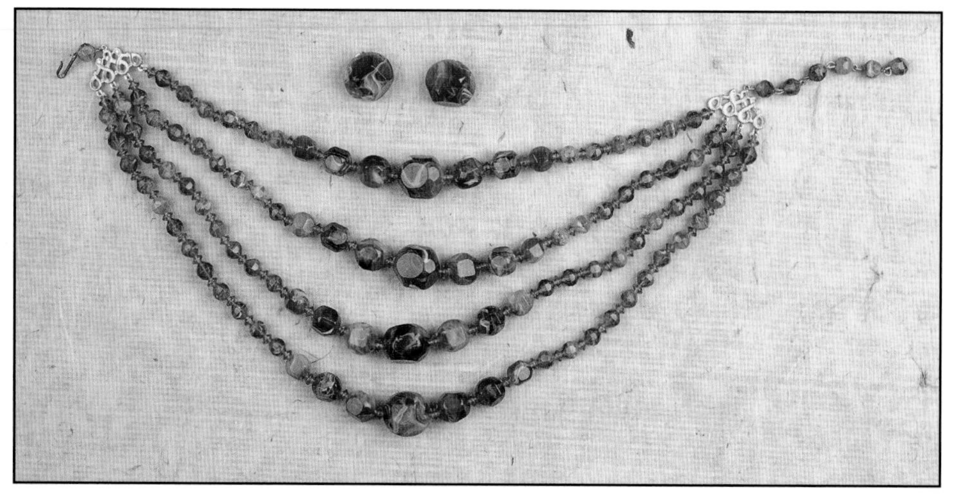

Triple strand Lucite and thermoplastic bead necklace and earring set in lilac and white is perfect for springtime wear. $40-50 set.

Huge three-strand faceted and graduated Lucite bead necklace in varying shades of purple and accented with gold-tone spacer beads. $60-75.

Choker necklace, elastic bracelet and clip earrings were designed with faceted Lucite beads in amber and lavender. $20-50 each.

Two bracelets and matching choker necklace made of root beer colored Lucite. $35-50 each.

Wonderfully shaped Lucite beads which were faceted as well as graduated were used to create this double strand necklace and earring set in amber and root beer tones. $65-85 set.

Two-toned pink necklace and funky flower pins all made of Lucite. $35-65 each.

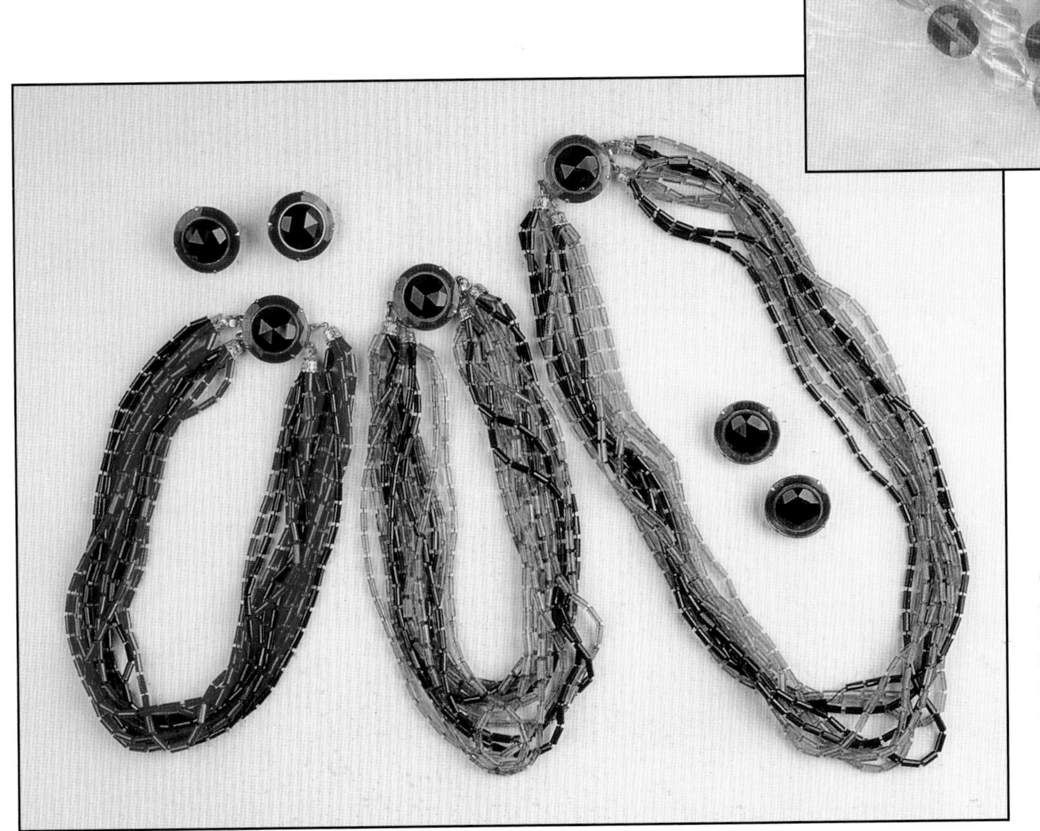

Olive green, amber and candy apple red plastic was accented with black to create stunning multi-strand necklace and earring sets. $45-65 each set.

Lucite and Bakelite necklaces designed with transparent and opaque beads in lovely earth tone colors. $40-95 each.

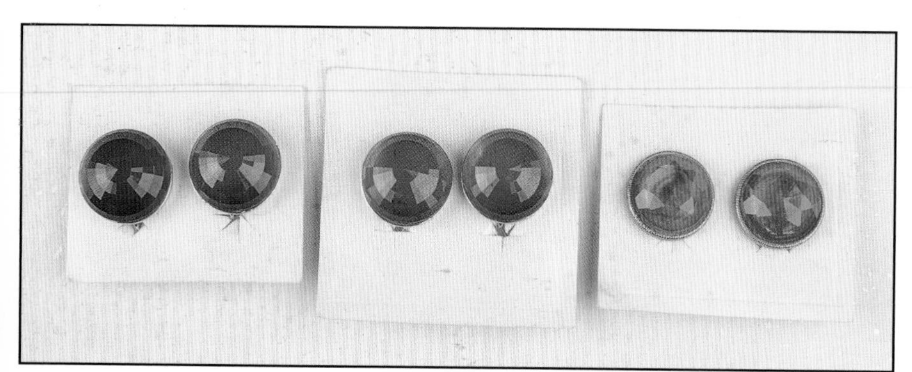

Faceted Lucite earrings in blue, green and orange. $20-30 each pair.

Close-up of clear faceted Lucite earrings resembling crystal or glass. $20-30.

Colorful and fun assortment of clip-on earrings made of thermoset plastic as well as Lucite. $25-35 each pair.

Clusters of molded leaves and rose beads were used to create these mid-century plastic clip-on earrings. $30-40 each pair.

Chapter 3
Late in the Century

Natural Materials

By the early 1970s, metal jewelry was quite common and accented with wood, cork, glass and plastic beads. Real amber jewelry became the height of fashion in the mid-1970s, with necklaces, designed by Les Bernard, of pale opaque yellow to honey-colored amber from the Baltic Sea. This line of jewelry also consisted of genuine coral, horn, mother-of-pearl and jade. Synthetics followed the lead of the natural substances and tons of inexpensive plastic jewelry was mass-produced to rival the look of the real thing.

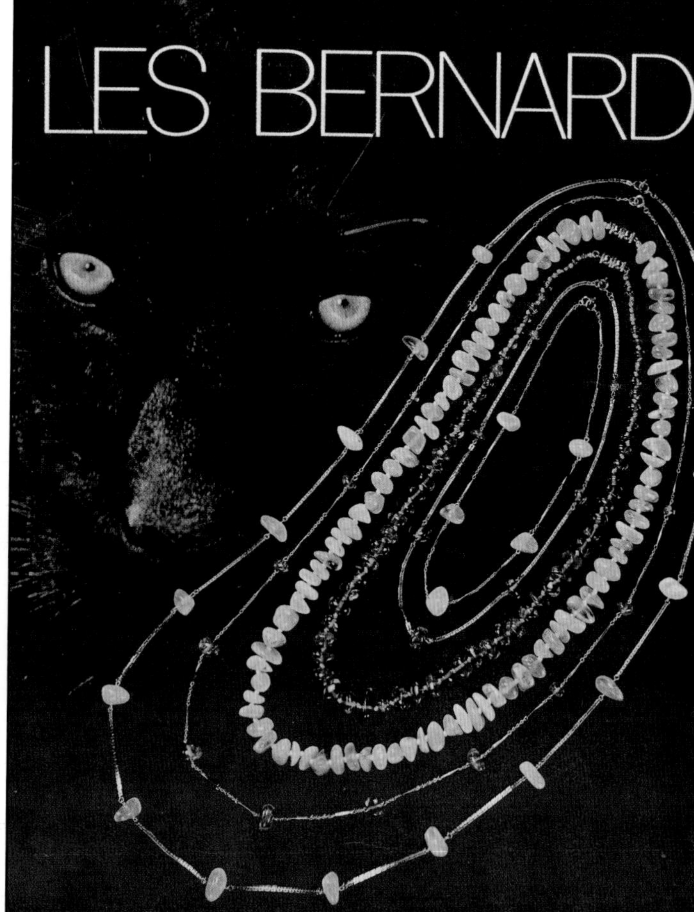

A natural plastic, amber, was used to create these wonderful necklaces by Les Bernard in 1974. The real Baltic amber ranged in color from pale opaque yellow to dark honey color. They ranged in price at that time from $15 to $75 each.

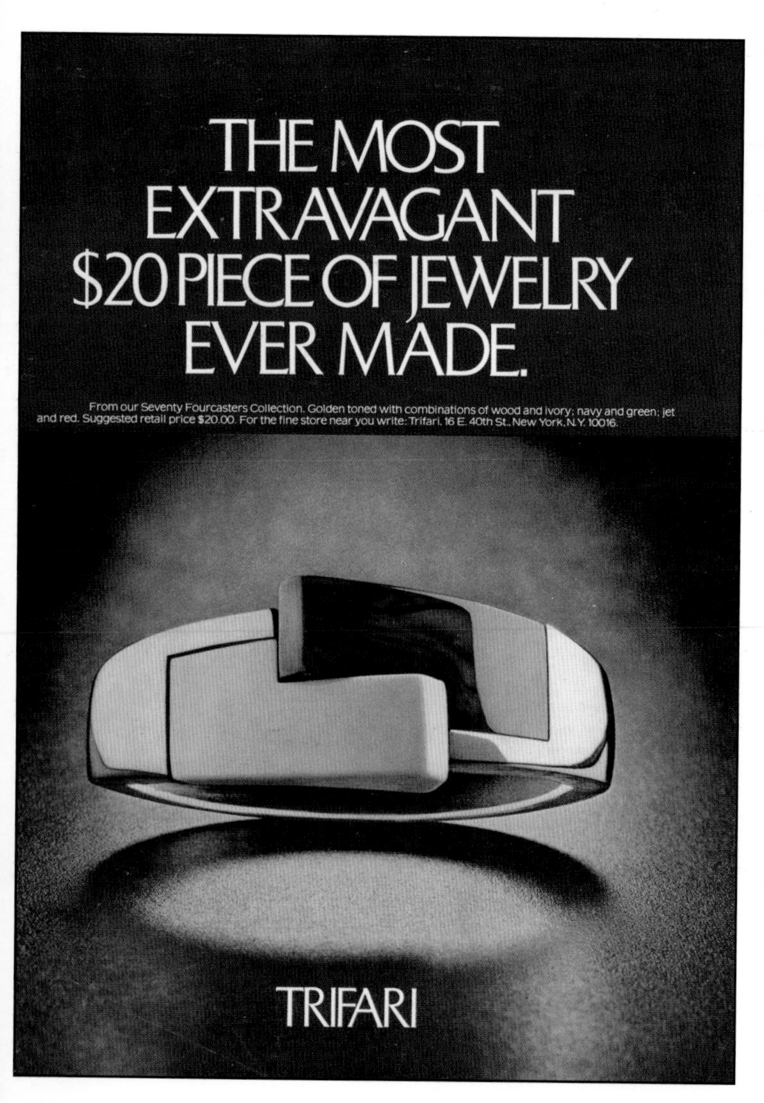

From the Seventy Fourcasters Collection, this Trifari bracelet was made with a combination of wood and plastic. It retailed for $20 in 1974.

Thermoset

By the late1970s and early1980s, designer Kenneth Jay Lane utilized clear and colored thermoset plastics in his designs, many of which were reminiscent of Art Deco styles of the 1930s. He also used thermoset plastics to imitate precious and semi-precious stones. Avon also created lines of jewelry utilizing synthetic plastics to resemble genuine stones and natural plastics.

Art Deco style plastic necklaces by Trifari; bracelet by Kenneth Jay Lane and crystal earrings by Eisenberg Ice, popular in 1972.

Realistic three-dimensional thermoset plastic flower brooch and earring set accented with rhinestones. $85-100 set.

Beads

Different methods of fabrication produced different effects creating unlimited variety of all types of jewelry and in all price ranges. In the 1990s, inexpensive novelty stores had racks upon racks of plastic bead necklaces, earrings and pins at low prices while upscale department stores sold better quality plastic jewelry at a higher price. Again, companies like Trifari, Monet and even 1928 Jewelry Company utilized plastic in its designs of wonderful costume jewelry.

Chunky plastic beads in orange and yellow compliment this bright colored floral shift and floppy hat from 1967.

Models wearing bright colored plastic beads and bangle bracelets, Vogue, May 1964.

Large fringed neckpiece made of plastic beads, Vogue, May 1964.

Thermoplastics

Throughout the 20th century, hundreds of different types of thermoplastics were created. Different plastics had different uses and technology kept improving.

This thermoplastic set looks almost like a fireworks display. $75-100 set.

Resins

Close to the end of the 20th century, different types of resins became common household words. Polyresins were common and inexpensive materials used for making figurines, picture frames, clocks, and a host of other decorative items for the home and garden. Some jewelry was made of resins, but the majority were inexpensive decorative objects that filled the shelves of dollar stores across the country. Many of these items were imported to the United States from China.

With this in mind, one can never tell what the plastics industry of the 21st century will hold. It might be a whole different ball game. Time will tell!

Although this was a vintage ad from 1967 for Dash laundry detergent, this model is really mod wearing oversized clear Lucite or possibly Plexiglas drop earrings.

Make-up ad with model wearing mod style plastic drop earrings and plastic bangle bracelets, Ladies' Home Journal, June 1966.

Opposite: double-crocheted dress with deep V back costs $11.56 to make (4 skeins of yarn, $5.56; 3 packages of sequins, $6). Earrings, Mimi di N. This page: iridescent halter dress costs $16.68 to make (12 skeins of yarn $4.68; 6 packages of sequins, $12). Earrings, Castlecliff. To order directions for making both dresses (and sweater on our cover) turn to page 100. All yarn by Coats & Clark; sequins by Sol Kahaner.

By Nora O'Leary, Patterns Editor

Photographs by Bill Helburn

61

Not only is this mod model wearing plastic earrings, her whole shift dress is covered in metallic pink plastic pailettes, Ladies' Home Journal, July 1966.

Mimi di N jeweled belt and oversized brooch sold through Bonwit Teller in 1968.

Ropes of long plastic pearls by Marvella advertised for sale in 1974.

From the Autumn Hues collection, this Trifari plastic pendant was a hit in 1973. It was available in tortoise, ivory, jade or lapis and retailed for $15.

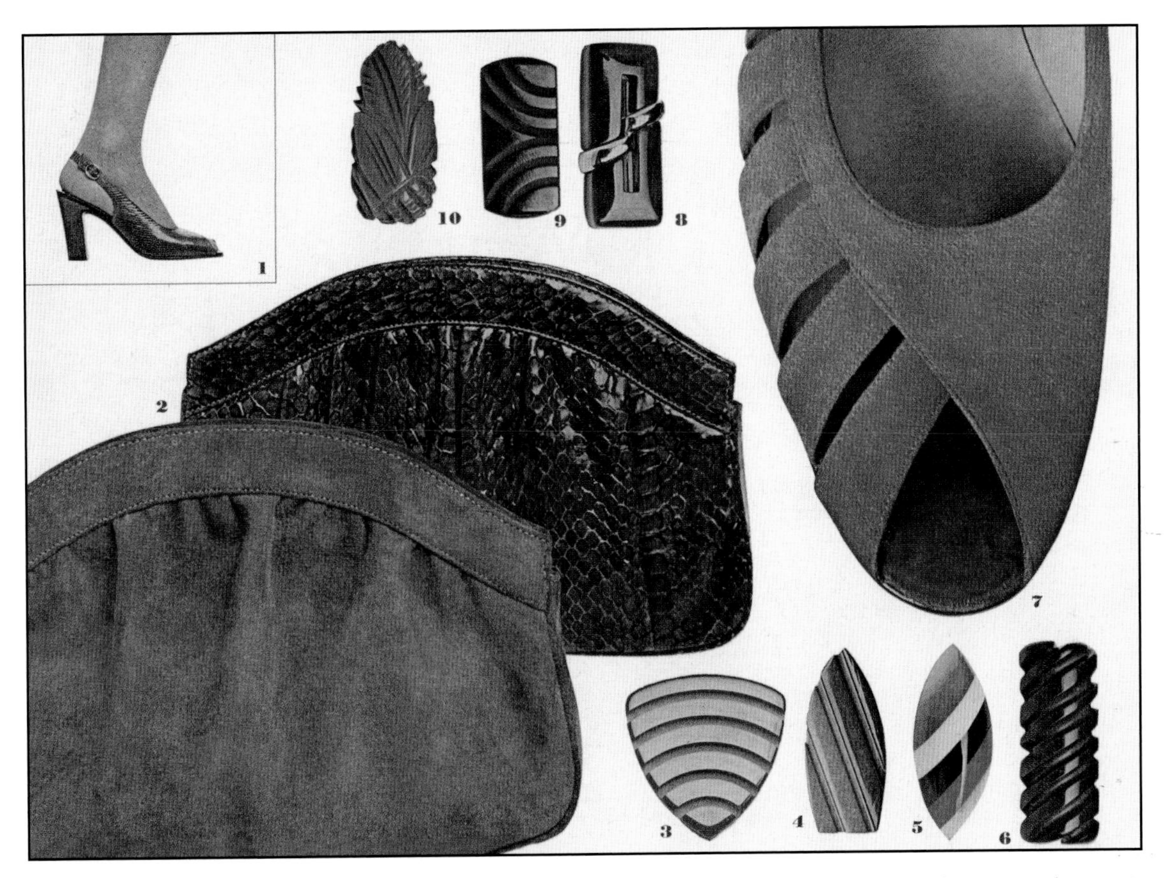

Plastic jewelry and accessories for the fall of 1974. Notice how the buckles and clips were made very similar to those of the Art Deco era. Pins and clips were advertised as must-have accessories to hold scarves and mufflers, to stick on a beret, at the waist of a skirt, on a dress.

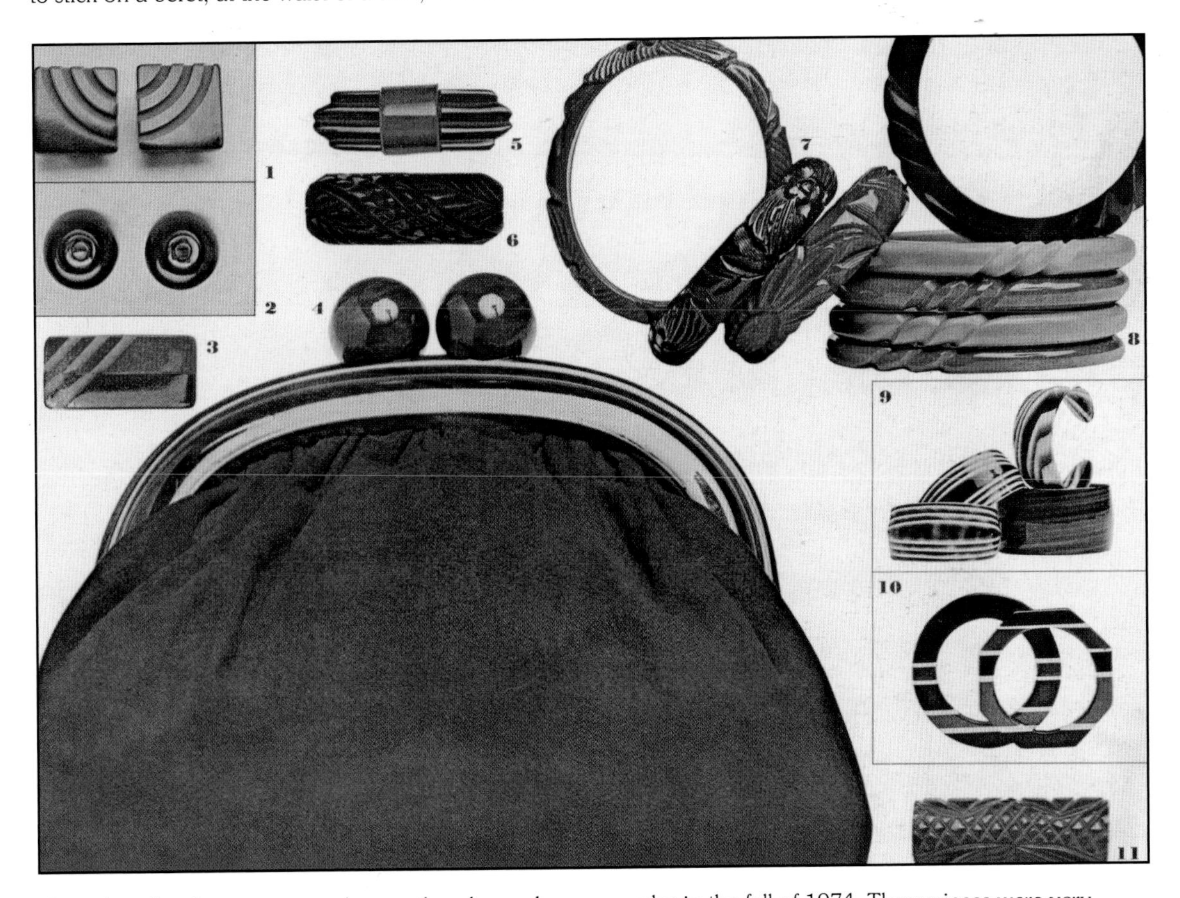

Plastic bangles that were carved, smooth or layered were popular in the fall of 1974. These pieces were very reminiscent of the 1930s. Earth tone colors were in vogue.

Big chunky necklaces by Arpad for Hattie Carnegie in 1964.

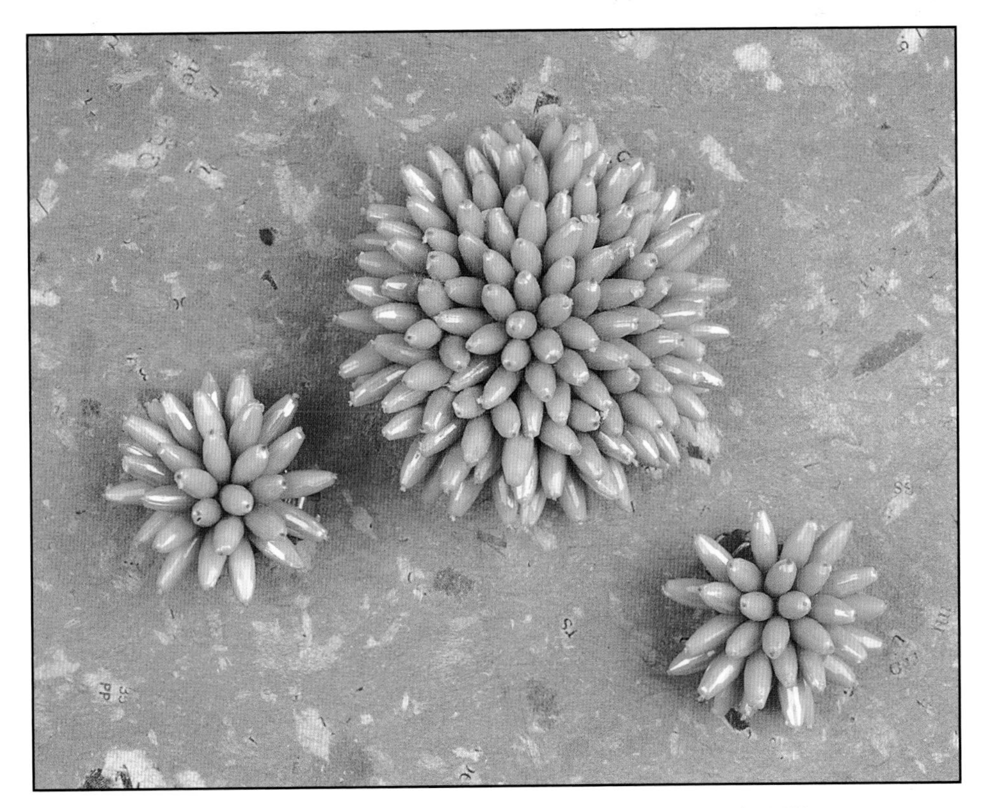

Stylized flower brooch and matching earrings made of lavender plastic. $50-75 set.

Mod brooches in brightly colored Lucite, Hong Kong. $30-65 each.

Atomic style jewelry made of two-toned Plexiglass. $65-85 set.

More atomic style pin and earring sets made of plastic in purple and green. $75-90 each set.

The atomic style is evident in these brightly colored plastic brooches and multi-strand necklace. $35-50 each.

Laminated plastic pendant strung on a silk cord. $75-100.

Stacks of plastic and Lucite polka dot and rhinestone-studded bangle bracelets. $100-200 each.

Mod rings made of varying plastics from the 1960s in assorted styles and colors. $50-75 each.

Lucite and Bakelite rings in assorted colors and styles. $50-85 each.

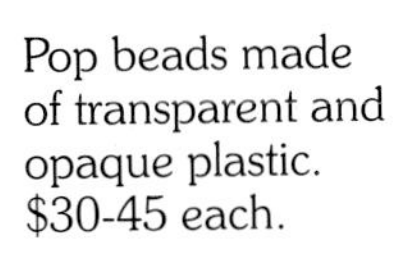

Pop beads made of transparent and opaque plastic. $30-45 each.

Transparent, metallic and confetti Lucite bangle bracelets ranging in size from very thin to extremely wide. $50-200 each.

Mod earrings by designer Paco Rabanne made of thin strips of plastic. $85-100 pair.

Colored plastic bangles with brass studs and earrings to match. $40-95 each.

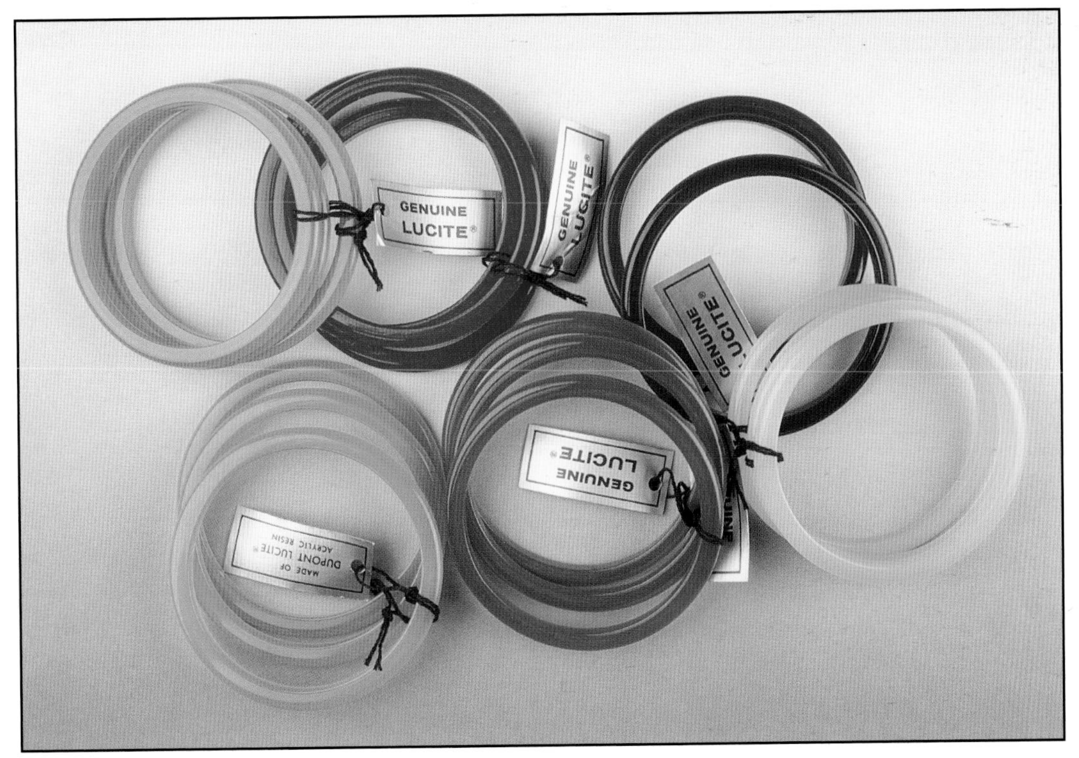

Brightly-colored bangle bracelets in sets of three, still retaining their original tags which read "Made of Dupont Lucite Acrylic Resin". $25-35 each set.

Chunky necklace of brass-studded Lucite beads. $75.00.

A beautiful combination of chunky pastel pink plastic beads and large silvertone textured links created a lovely demi-parure by Napier. $145 set.

Long lariat style necklace and matching dangle earrings made with goldtone links and faceted white plastic beads. $95 set.

Mod necklaces made with unusual shaped black and white plastic beads. $65 each.

Large and funky yellow and purple twisted plastic dangle earrings. $55.

Mod earrings in geometric shapes made of Lucite. $50-65 each pair.

Dangles, clusters and shoulder dusters in Lucite, Bakelite and thermoplastic. $45-75 each pair.

Mod and geometric earrings in assorted plastics. $35-48 each pair.

Hoop earrings made of assorted colors of Bakelite. $45-65 each pair.

Mod thermoset plastic necklaces and clip earrings in two-toned color combinations. $30-65 each.

Novelty pins with food themes made of thermoset plastic. $25-35 each.

Whimsical mod brooches made of thermoset plastic in wonderful color combinations, W. Germany. $35-45 each.

Tiny novelty scatter pins in red and black thermoplastic accented with rhinestones. $15-25 each.

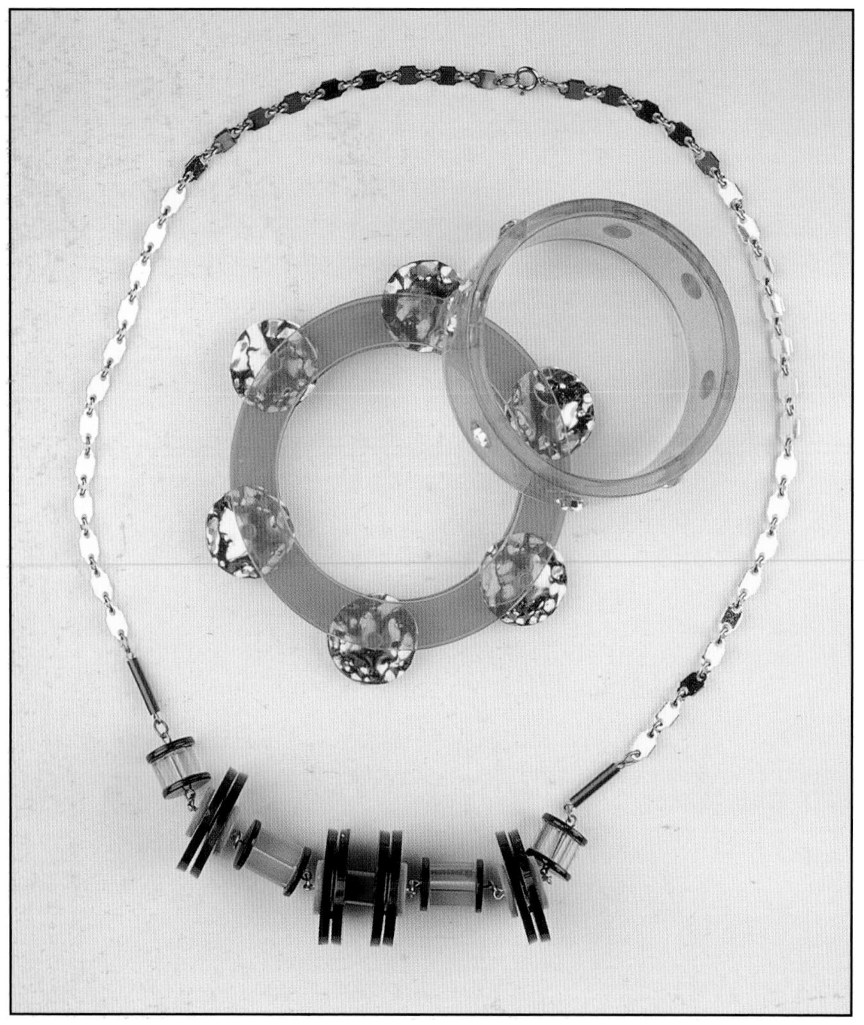

Necklace and bangle bracelets, Lucite with metal and rhinestone accents. $40-75 each.

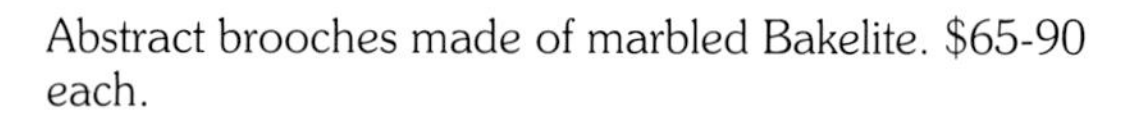

Abstract brooches made of marbled Bakelite. $65-90 each.

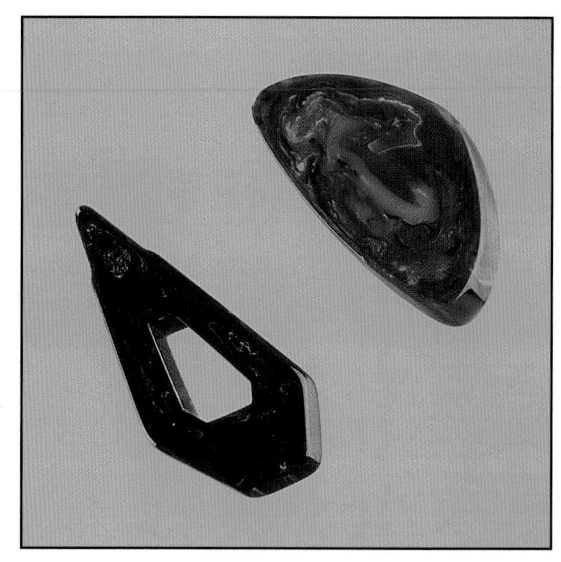

Plastic bead necklace with goldtone spacers. $65.

Pink and red stacked plastic bead necklace, Trifari. $85.

Assorted plastic beads and textured goldtone spacers created a lovely necklace by Freirich. $95.

Chunky charm bracelet, plastic and metal, unmarked. $95.

Two chunky charm bracelets overflowing with white plastic beads in assorted geometric shapes. $75 each.

Two unusual bangle bracelets; one made of a mirrored plastic with a square shape and the second, a combination of plastic and wood. $50-85 each.

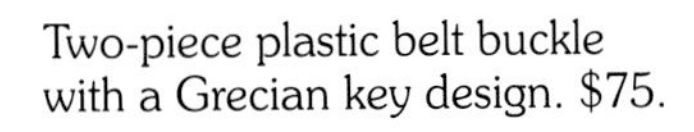

Two-piece plastic belt buckle with a Grecian key design. $75.

A spectacular three dimensional neckpiece of faux turquoise, goldtone imitation branch coral and Austrian crystal accents, Mimi di N. $1200-1500.

Oversized neckpiece with matching earrings designed with transparent plastic faceted beads, disks and links, unmarked. $350-400 set.

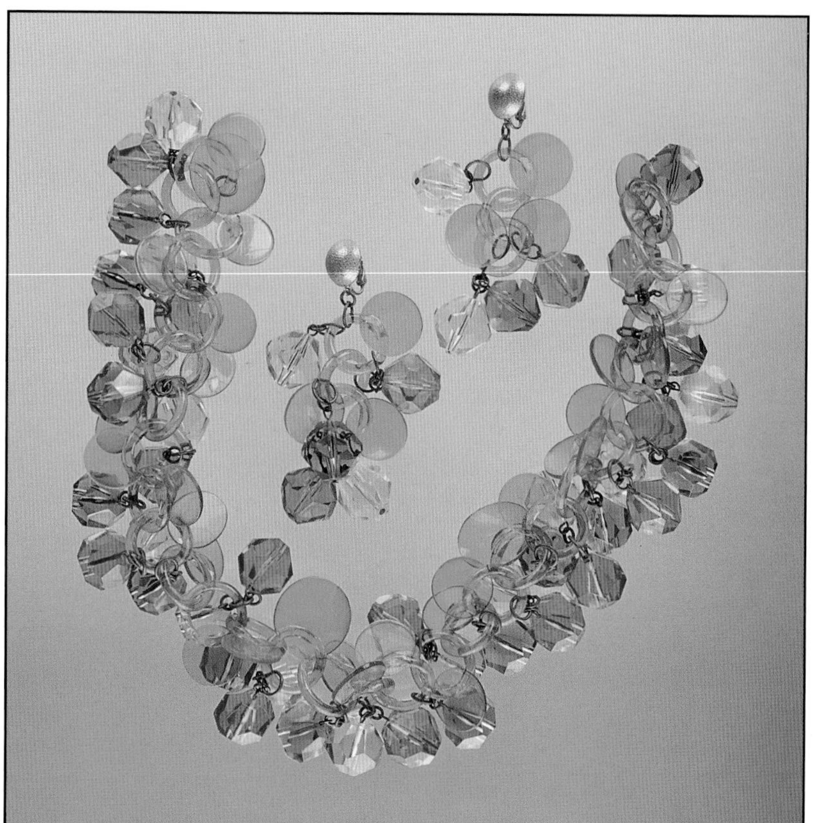

Bib necklaces and matching earrings made with emerald green and sapphire blue plastic beads. $150-200 each set.

Pale pink and clear Lucite bib necklaces designed with a variety of faceted beads creating a crystal-like appearance, Tatiana. $300-400 each.

Oversized fringed neckpiece with assorted beads in pale pink and clear acrylic made to imitate crystal. $350-450.

Multi-strand necklace with elongated green and purple plastic beads, Kramer. $125-150.

Lavender and red acrylic beads coupled with rhinestones, faux pearls and enamel created a winning combination on this lovely necklace signed Mimi di N. $200-250.

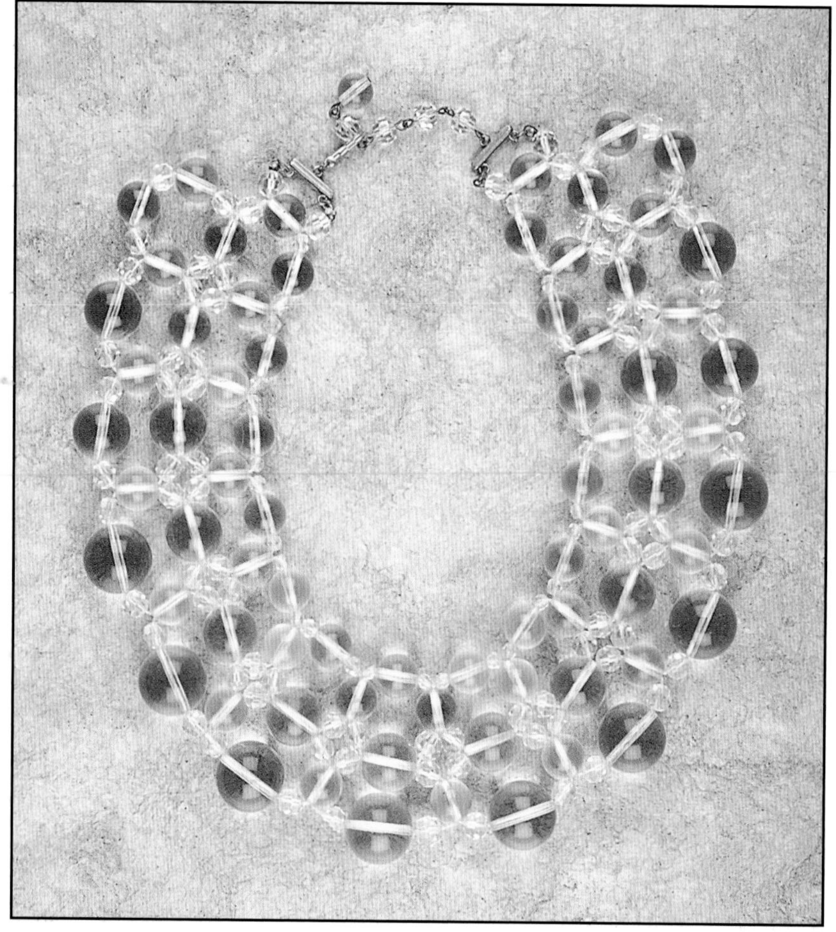

Unique lattice-style clear Lucite collar necklace, unmarked. $175-225.

Collar necklace made of amber-colored acrylic beads. $135-175.

Fringed necklace and matching bracelet with dangling white disks and rhinestone-studded flowers made of thermoplastic. $145-195 set.

Fringed necklace and earring set in grey and gold plastic beads accented with metal spacers. $115-145 set.

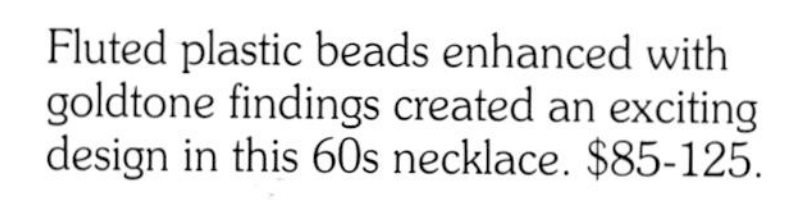

Fluted plastic beads enhanced with goldtone findings created an exciting design in this 60s necklace. $85-125.

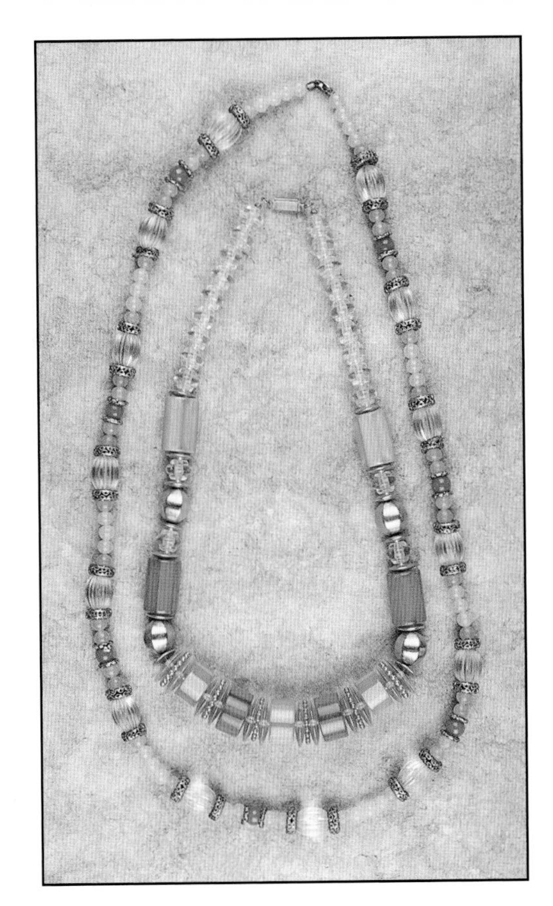

Two necklaces made of pastel-colored plastic beads. $60-90 each.

Scarab pendant necklace, metal and molded plastic, KJL. $150-200.

Choker necklace, metal and molded plastic, Donald Stannard. $75-95..

Pendant necklace, marbled Bakelite and metal. $145-195.

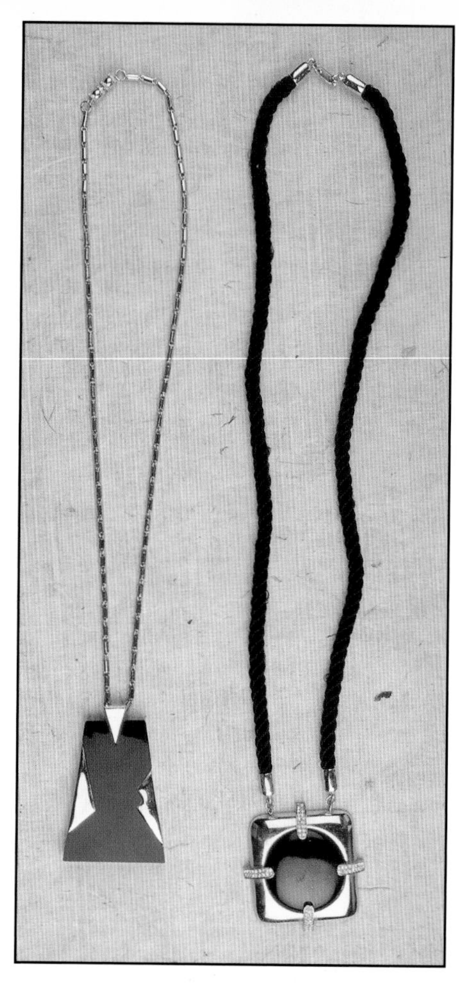

Art Deco style pendant necklaces in plastic and metal, Trifari and Castlecliff. $125-150 each.

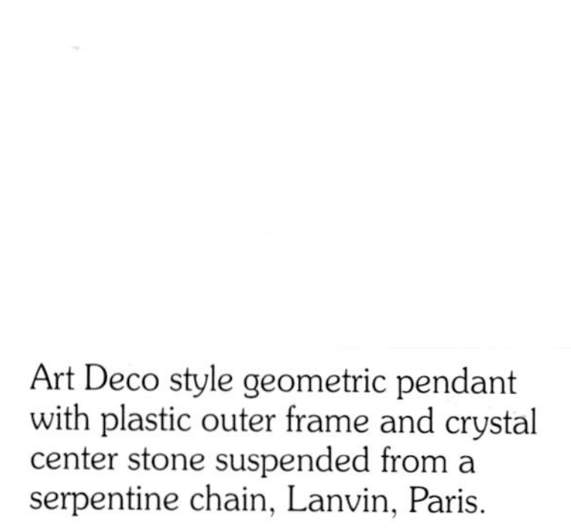

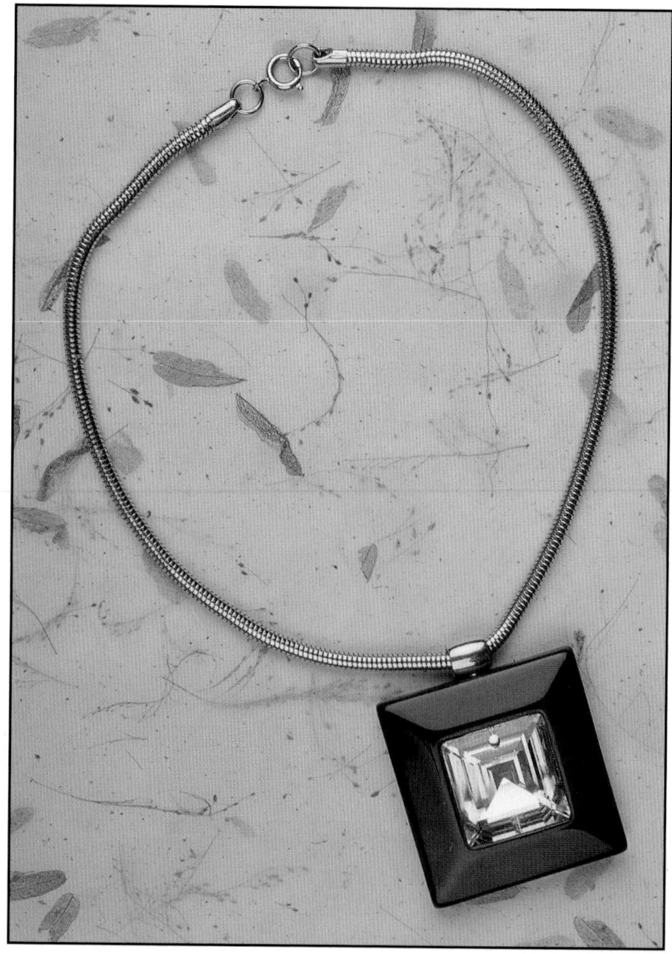

Art Deco style geometric pendant with plastic outer frame and crystal center stone suspended from a serpentine chain, Lanvin, Paris.

Bangle bracelets with rhinestone accents made of Lucite and Marblette. $45-125 each.

Art Deco style beaded necklace, faux pearls and Lucite. $85.

Fish pendant necklace, thermoplastic, metal and rhinestones. $145-175.

Oversized figural owl and rooster pins, plastic and metal, Hattie Carnegie. $145-195 each.

Pop art novelty necklace, sardines in a can, plastic, Hattie Carnegie. $150-200.

Oversized tri-color plastic heart suspended from a brown silk cord. $95.

Large pendant necklace, egg-shaped Lucite drop. $75.

Large plastic pendant made to resemble jade with an oriental motif. $125.

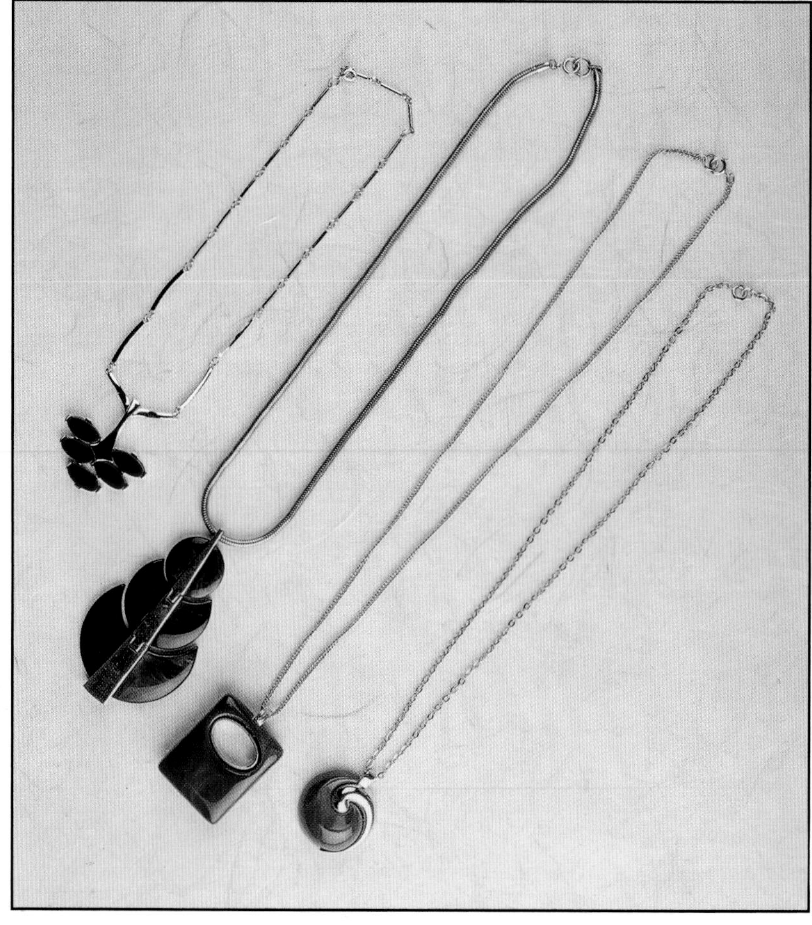

1970s vintage Art Deco style pendant necklaces made of plastic resembling Bakelite, Trifari and Sarah Coventry. $75-145 each.

Rhodium-plated pendant with dark blue plastic center, Lanvin, Paris. $135-150.

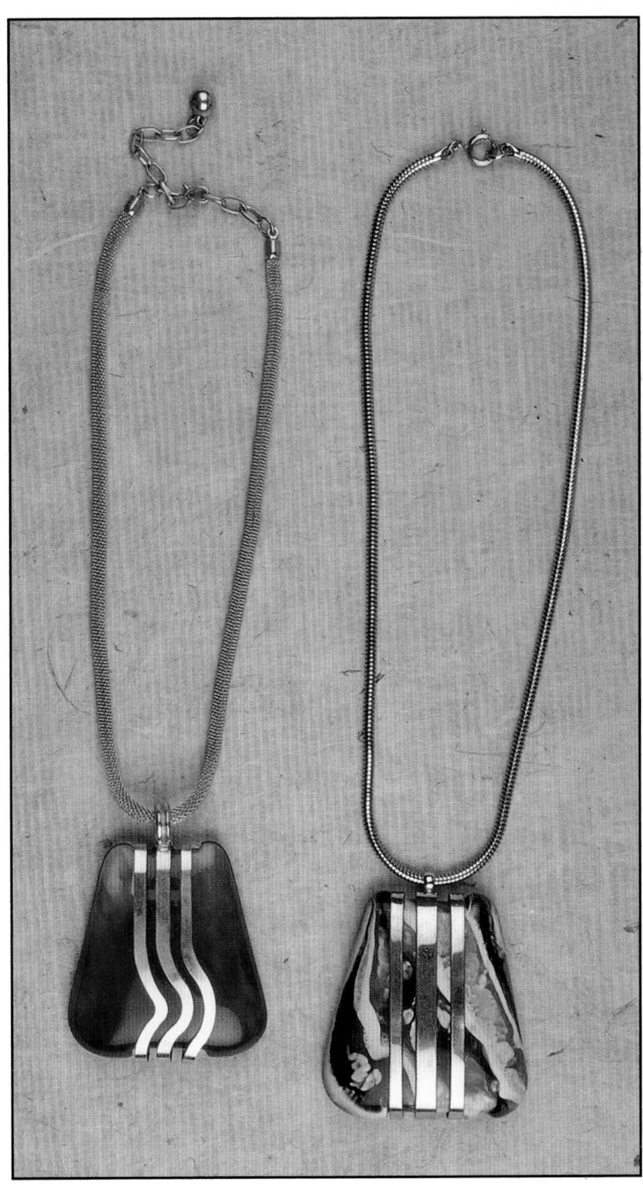

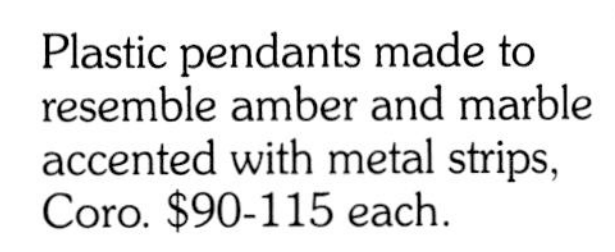

Plastic pendants made to resemble amber and marble accented with metal strips, Coro. $90-115 each.

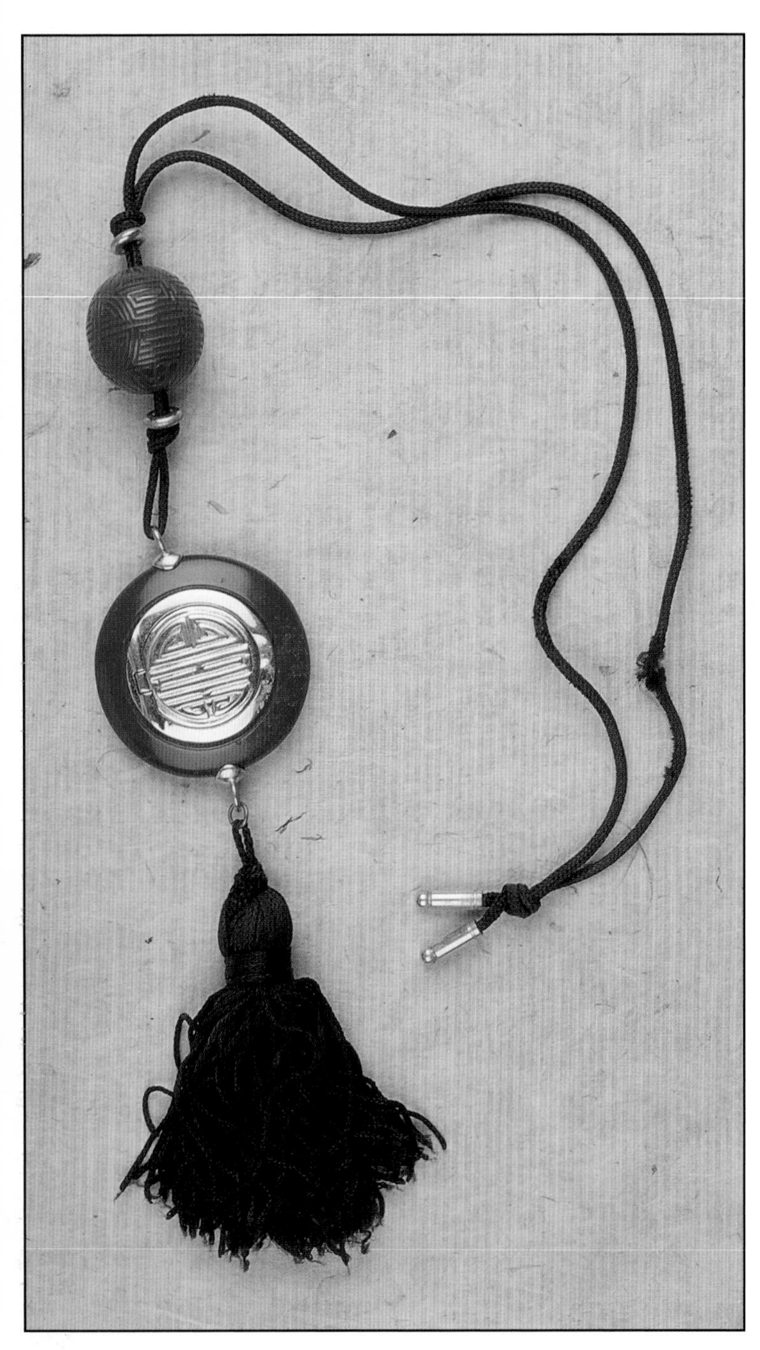

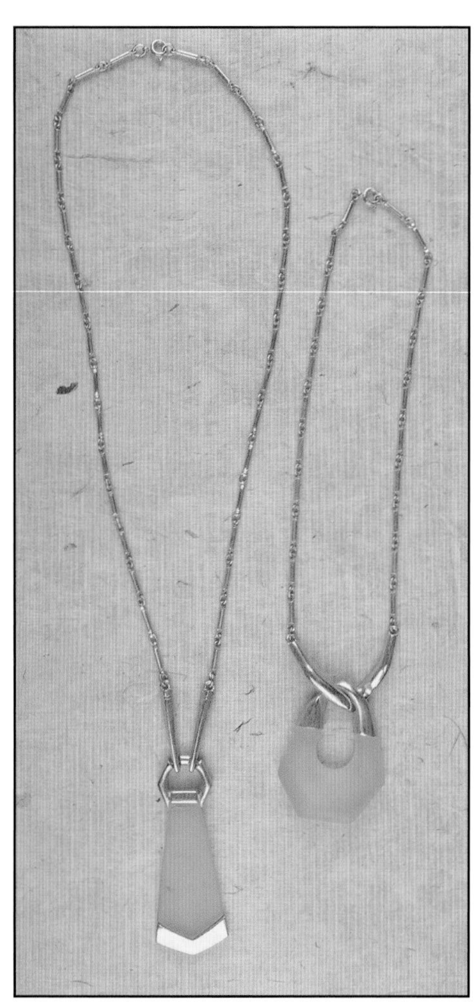

Two pendant necklaces, frosted plastic and goldtone metal. $65 each

Oriental style solid perfume pendant necklace made of plastic resembling cinnabar. $125.

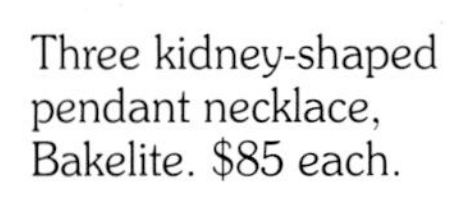

Three kidney-shaped pendant necklace, Bakelite. $85 each.

Patriotic red, white and blue plastic beads were further accented with Murano glass and goldtone fluted spacer beads creating a wonderful 70s design. $75-95.

More patriotic bead necklaces designed with glass and plastic. $35-50 each.

Molded plastic cameos and ribbon were used to create these elaborate brooches, earrings and belt. $100-150 set.

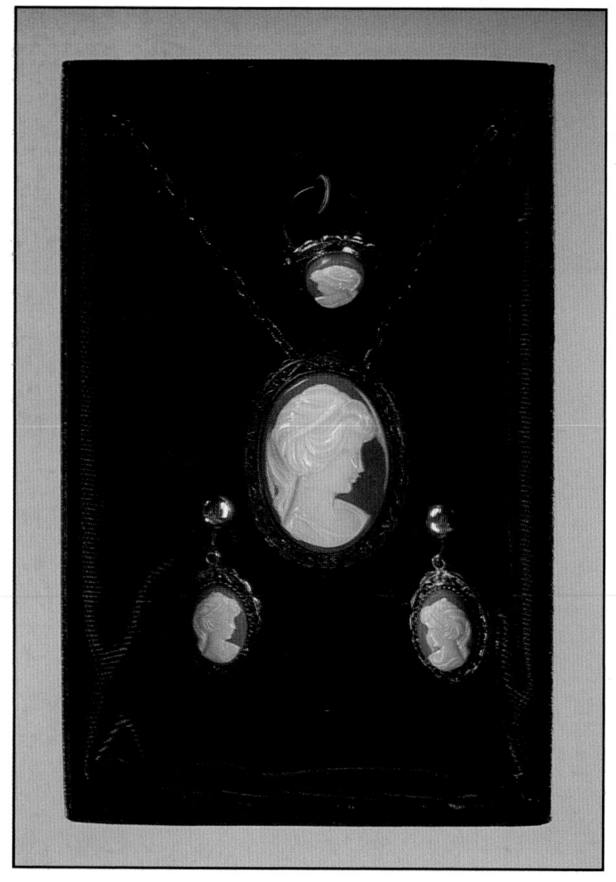

Molded plastic cameo parure by Peri. $40-65 set.

Molded plastic cameo jewelry by Peri. $20-45 each.

Charming pink and black plastic hearts dangle from black chain to form a wonderful pin and earring set by Miriam Haskell. $295-350 set.

Plastic cherry jewelry, Red Cobra by Frank Giordano. $75-150 each.

More whimsical plastic fruit jewelry, Red Cobra by Frank Giordano. $60-85 each.

Plastic leaf necklace, Red Cobra by Frank Giordano. $50-75.

Multi-colored plastic charm necklace with fish theme and hand-painted accents, Red Cobra by Frank Giordano. $85-125.

Fun plastic necklaces utilizing multi-color beads, striped rings and cotton cord, Red Cobra by Frank Giordano. $50-75 each.

Lucky charm necklace made of red, white and black plastic, Red Cobra by Frank Giordano. $60-80.

Domino and dice necklace made of red, white and black plastic, Red Cobra by Frank Giordano. $45-65.

Choker necklace made of hearts, spades, diamonds and clubs in plastic, Red Cobra by Frank Giordano. $50-75.

Necklaces made of stripes and polka dots in plastic with strands of twisted cord and beaded chains, Red Cobra by Frank Giordano. $45-65 each.

Art Deco style plastic necklace with fan-shaped pendant and rhinestone accents. $45-75.

Polka dot beads add a touch of whimsy to these black and white beaded necklaces made of plastic. $35-50 each.

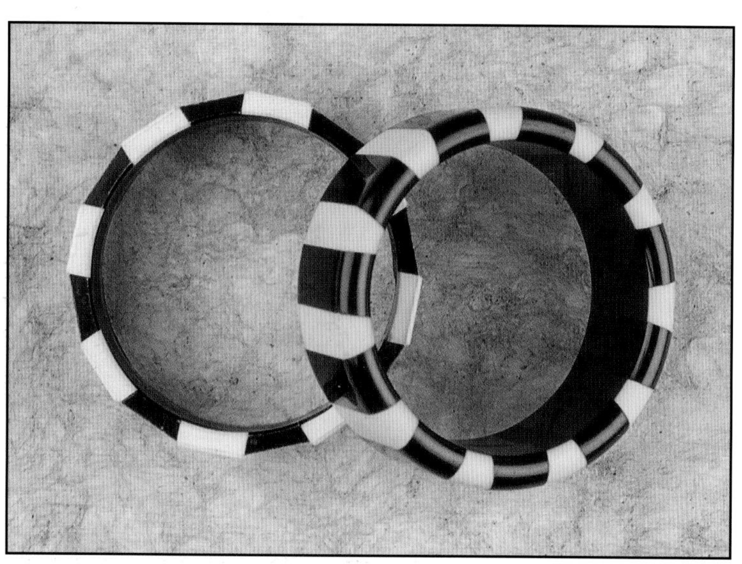

Bangle bracelets in alternating light and dark plastics. $50-75 each.

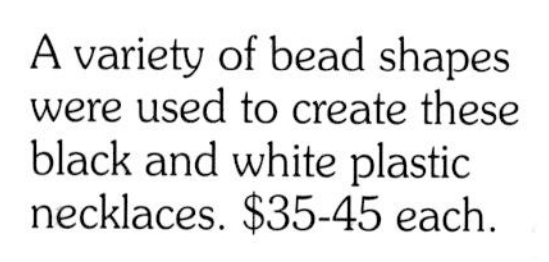

A variety of bead shapes were used to create these black and white plastic necklaces. $35-45 each.

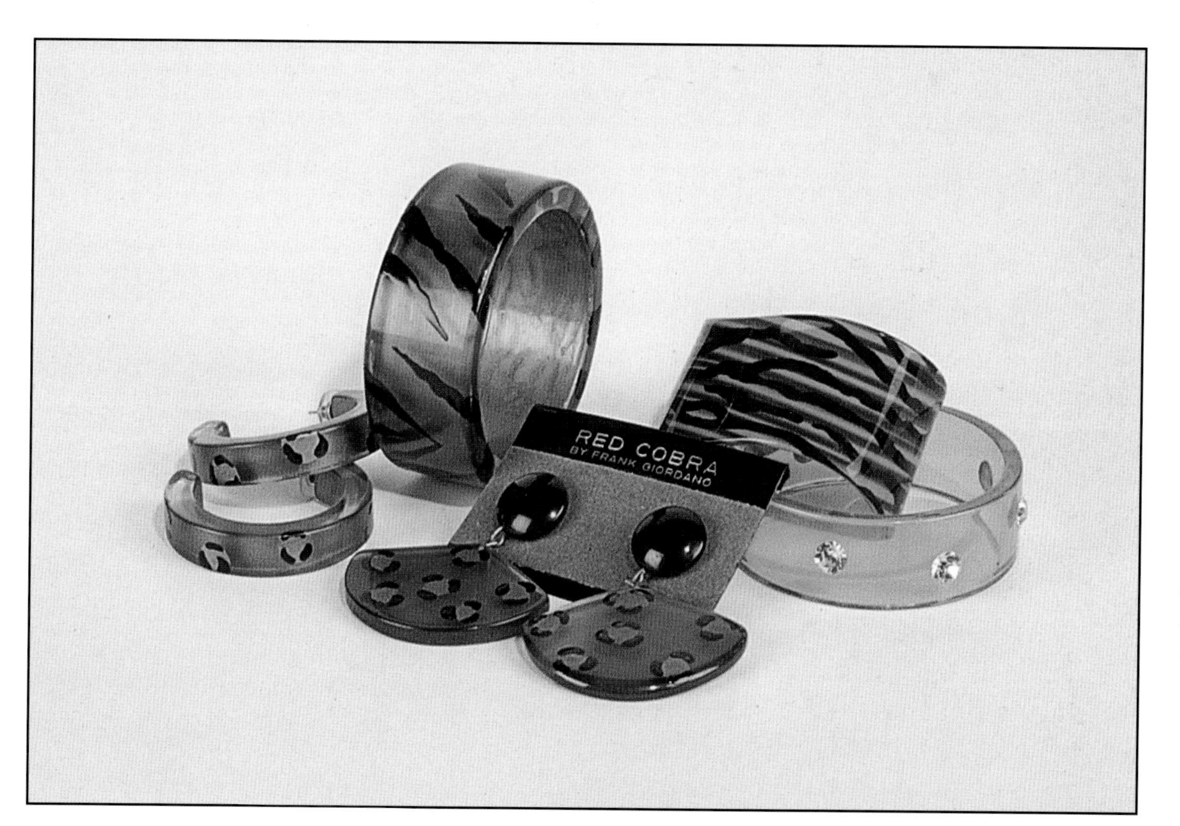

Animal prints transformed into plastic bangles and earrings; rhinestone studded bangle bracelet in transparent Lucite. $40-85 each.

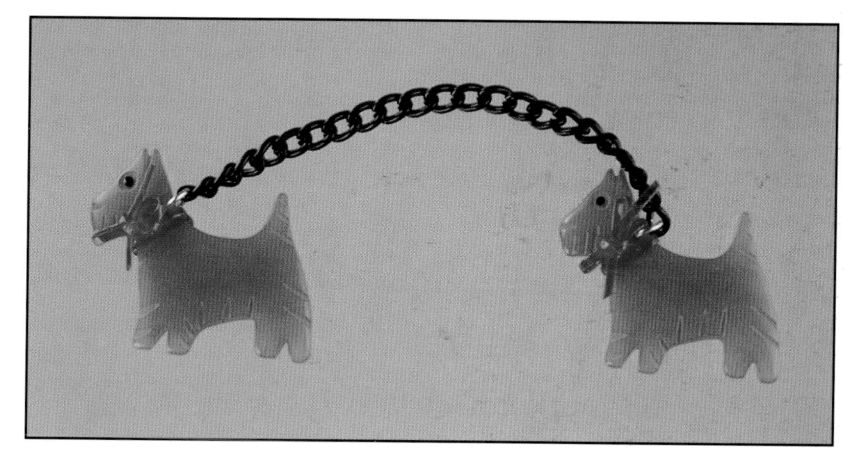

Plastic scottie dog pins decorated with red bows and connected by black chain, Miriam Haskell. $100-150.

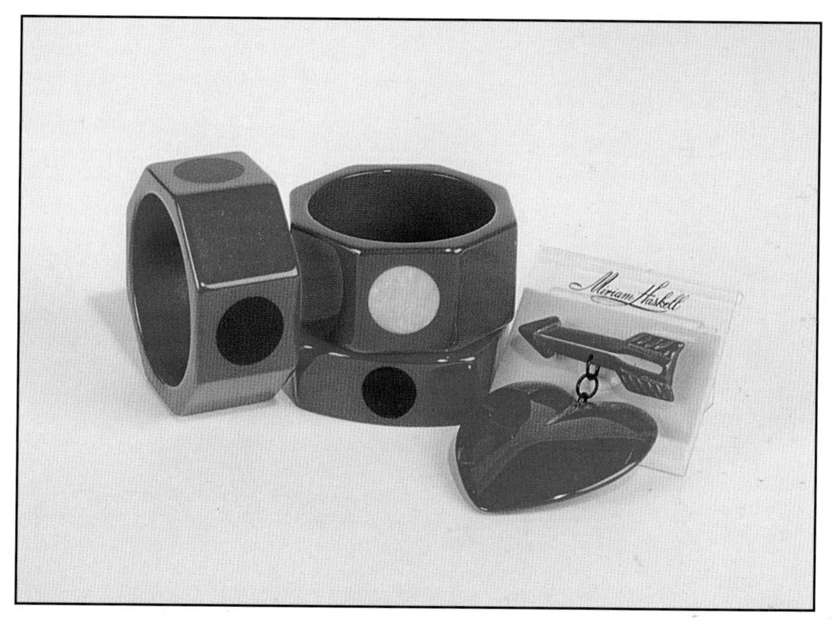

Polka dot bangles and heart and arrow brooch, Miriam Haskell. $250-350 each.

Light blue plastic parure with smooth and faceted beads and gold-plated accents, Napier. $70-90 set.

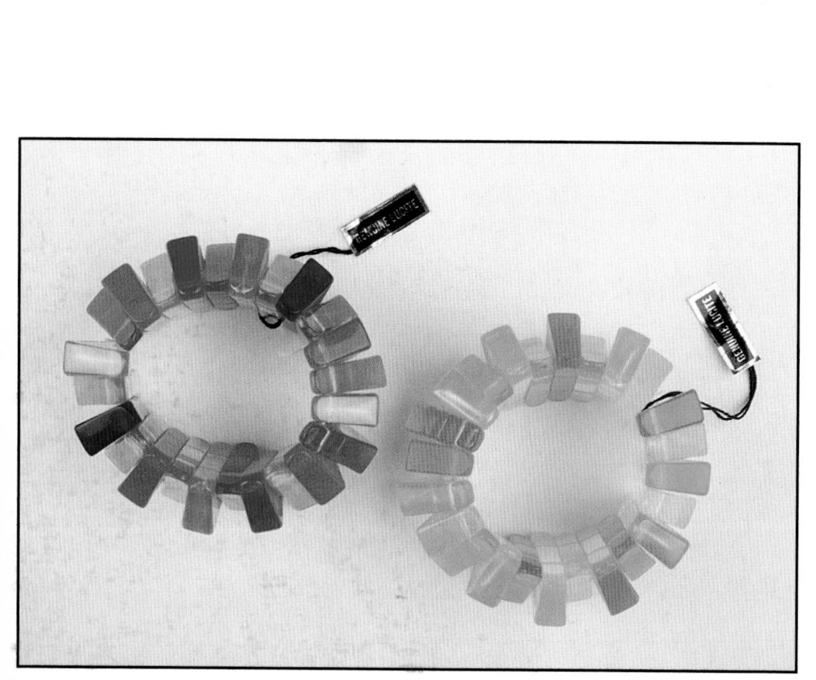

Genuine Lucite stretch bracelets in shades of blue and pink. $60-85 each.

Tri-colored triple strand Lucite necklace. $48-65.

Bibliography

Books

Baker, Lillian. *Plastic Jewelry of the Twentieth Century.* Paducah, Kentucky: Collector Books, 2003.

Burkholtz, Matthew. *The Bakelite Collection*. Atglen, Pennsylvania: Schiffer Publishing Ltd., 1997.

Ettinger, Roseann. *Antique Dresser Sets, 1890-1950s.* Atglen, Pennsylvania: Schiffer Publishing Ltd., 2005.

Klein, Susan Maxine. *Mid-Century Plastic Jewelry.* Atglen, Pennsylvania: Schiffer Publishing Ltd., 2005.

Leshner, Leigh. *Collecting Art Plastic Jewelry. Iola, Wisconsin:* kp books, 2005.

Lindenberger, Jan. *Collecting Plastics, A Handbook & Price Guide.* Atglen, Pennsylvania: Schiffer Publishing Ltd., 1991.

McNulty, Lyndi Stewart. *Price Guide to Plastic Collectibles.* Radnor, Pennsylvania: Wallace Homestead Book Company, 1992.

Modern Plastics Encyclopedia, Charles A. Breskin, Publisher, 1949.

Modern Plastics Encyclopedia, Stuart S. Siegel, Publisher, 1977-78.

Romero, Christie. *Warman's Jewelry, Identification and Price Guide.* Iola, Wisconsin: Krause Publications, 2002.

Magazines

Charm, April, 1955, November, 1956.

Glamour, December, 1954, March, 1957.

Ladies' Home Journal, June and July, 1966.

Mademoiselle, August, 1954.

McCall's, October, 1967.

Seventeen, November, 1946 and May, 1967.

Vogue, June, 1956, May and June, 1960, May, 1961, 1962, 1963 and 1964, September, 1968, August and September, 1972, 1973 and 1974.

Catalogs

A. Hirsch Co., Wholesale Jewelers, Chicago, Ill., 1931. Butler Brothers, New York, 1937.

Jewel Creations, 1960.

L & C Mayers, New York, 1958.

National Cloak & Suit Company, New York, 1925.

Sears, Roebuck & Company, Chicago, Ill., 1937, 1938, 1939.

Index